Pearl Harbor Story

MAJOR GENERAL H. D. RUSSELL

Pearl Harbor Story

By

Henry Dozier Russell

Mercer University Press
Memorial Day
2001

ISBN 0-86554-769-6
MUP/P222

Published by
Mercer University Press
6316 Peake Road
Macon, Georgia 31210-3960

First Edition.

∞The paper used in this publication meets the minimum requirements of American
National Standard for Information Sciences—Permanence of Paper for Printed
Library Materials, ANSI Z39.48-1992.

Library of Congress Cataloging-in-Publication Data

CIP data are available from the Library of Congress

Contents

Foreword

Major General H. D. Russell was a member of the U. S. Army Pearl Harbor Investigation Board which completed its work in October 1944. He dictated his recollection of that experience early in 1946, soon after his return to civilian life following six years of active duty with the Army. We do not know when his dictation was transcribed. A few handwritten corrections had been made. A few carbon copies circulated among his friends and relatives during his lifetime.

When the investigation ended, all the information gathered by the Board was classified "Top Secret" by the U. S. War Department. Board members were ordered not to disclose any information about the investigation. In the preface to his dictation, General Russell recorded his response to that order: "In plain and vigorous language, I told (him) that I would express myself freely about Pearl Harbor if I desired when the War ended." With the adoption of the *Freedom of Information Act* in 1986 (USCA 5:552), even the Top Secret report of the Board is now available on the Internet.

The freshness of General Russell's recollection and the immediacy of the dictated style so near in time to the events make this account a valuable resource, even though some of the information is not now new to scholars.

Quite by chance in 1998, David L. Mincey, a Macon, Georgia, lawyer and World War II Navy combat veteran, came into possession of one of the carbon copies that have been lying around in cabinets and closets these 54 years. He recognized its historical significance and learned that it had not been published. He then found us, the Russell nieces who were the residual beneficiaries of our uncle's Will. We had long ago acted to protect the integrity of the text by having it copyrighted in our names. We had also placed one of the copies in the Archive of Contemporary History at the University of Wyoming.

But it is David L. Mincey whose interest, ability, diligence, and hard work made this fragile manuscript available to wider audiences.

His good secretary, Donna Hicks, patiently punched the fading words into her computer so as to produce a "clean copy" on good paper that is much easier to read. All of us were in agreement that the text should be published without editing and without comment, just as it was dictated early in 1946.

We are pleased that Mercer University Press is publishing this manuscript and making its availability known to both academic and general audiences through the marvels of the electronic age.

—Mary Russell Mitchell
—Frances Russell Furlow Jameson
December 7, 2000

Preface

I was a member of the Board appointed by the Secretary of War to investigate the Japanese attack at Pearl Harbor on December 7, 1941.

Before the investigation began, I discussed my assignment to the Board with G-1 of the General Staff. To that officer I expressed my wish to be relieved from the duty as vigorously as I could. So far as I know, no one in the Army wanted any part of the investigation. It was regarded as a highly undesirable job.

I was told that my selection for the Board was dictated by the desire of the War Department to have a lawyer with a military background as a member.

My interest was aroused by a statement that the Board's report would probably be made public. In and out of the Service there was a feeling that the entire truth about Pearl Harbor had never been told. I was in disagreement with this sentiment. I was commanding a division at Fort Jackson on December 7, 1941, and was busy at the time of the attack, for which reason I read the Roberts Report hastily, and assumed that the factual findings in that report were accurate and the conclusions sound. Nevertheless, the suspicion of the public grew and I felt that a thorough investigation, with full publicity for the report, might serve a useful purpose.

When the investigation was partially completed, a very disillusioning development occurred. As reported to the Board by Lt. Gen. Grunert, President of the Board, it was about as follows:

> Secretary of War Stimson was in New York for a week-end visit. He called General Grunert on the telephone and directed the utmost secrecy in connection with the Board's investigation. He was emphatic in his statement that no member of the Board or any one connected with it should release information of any kind to any one. All statements to the public would be made by the War Department through the proper officers.

There was nothing new about these instructions. They outlined a procedure which the Board had been following for approximately two months. To me the reasons for these instructions were clear. The pattern of the investigation at this time pointed to War Department derelictions. That Department had decided that findings against it would be made public when and under such circumstances as it determined, if as a matter of fact they were ever published.

Whatever doubt may have existed, as to the War Department intentions, was dispelled when the investigation ended. The Board and all those connected with it were required to sign a certificate or affidavit, that they had kept no notes and would not disclose any information obtained during the investigation. The presentation of the certificate was not without a kind of Gestapo technique. Major Clausen represented the War Department. He had several books on his desk, apparently Army regulations and others. They were either open or had markers in them. When he called me to execute the certificate he pointed to these books and stated that they were the authority requiring that we sign.

In plain and vigorous language, I told him that I would express myself freely about Pearl Harbor if I desired, when the War ended. In all events, since we were sworn to secrecy allegedly to protect the Japanese Code, which is now a matter of common knowledge, no reason for continued secrecy exists.

We submitted two reports, the one which was finally released by the President, and the other which has never been released. The one which the President made public was prepared so that it could have been published the day that it was completed, to wit; October 20, 1944. It was written for that purpose. The Japanese Code was protected fully. Our report went no further in divulging secrets than did the Roberts Report, which was given to the press immediately after its completion. The Roberts Report was released to the public because it vindicated Washington. Our report was withheld from the public because it charged derelictions to Washington. Statements that it was kept secret for security reasons are false.

On the 29th day of August, 1945, at 11 A.M., the President handed assembled newspapermen the text of the reports of the Army and Navy Boards for release at 1 P.M. that day. At the same time he gave the reporters a statement from Secretary Stimson, and his own statement.

I was then on duty at Columbus, Ohio. Two afternoon papers are published in that city. Their front page headlines were:

THE DISPATCH: "PEARL HARBOR REPORT HITS MARSHALL. FINDING IS UNJUSTIFIED SAYS TRUMAN. PRESIDENT SIDES WITH STIMSON IN DEFENDING CHIEF.

On Page 6-a of that paper, where the story was continued, the headline was: "TRUMAN DEFENDS MARSHALL, HIT IN PEARL HARBOR FINDINGS."

THE CITIZEN: "MARSHALL AND STARK ACCUSED OF NEGLECT IN ARMY AND NAVY REPORT. SHARE BLAME WITH HULL, SHORT AND KIMMEL. TRUMAN, STIMSON TAKE SHARP EXCEPTIONS.

In the story in *The Citizen*, attention is called to the fact that the President and the Secretary of War defended Marshall, but not Stark, whose derelictions were identical with those of Marshall.

In the stories, prominence was given to the defense of Marshall. The climax of this defense was contained in the statement by the President:

The conclusion of the Secretary of War is that General Marshall acted throughout this matter with his usual great skill, energy and efficiency. I associate myself wholeheartedly with this expression by the Secretary of War.

The President and Mr. Stimson intended and attempted to convey to the American people that General Marshall exhibited great skill, energy and efficiency in the Pearl Harbor affair. Thus construed, the statement is silly and ridiculous. The Secretary of War actually said that Marshall acted "with his usual great skill, energy and efficiency." If the Secretary had meant to convey the idea that

Marshall's conduct in the Pearl Harbor affair was characteristically Marshall, I have no quarrel with the statement.

Very little was said in the stories about the Board's findings. The criticism of those findings was featured. In a small way, the President and the Secretary of War defended Mr. Hull, but Marshall was the one to whose rescue they both went in a big way. Poor old Stark was completely forgotten.

My great faith in the Press was a little shaken. I investigated, asking two local editors at Columbus, Ohio, what they knew about our reports when they prepared editorials defending Marshall. One had the service of the Associated Press, the other the United Press. I have seen the stories dispatched by those two services. Both feature the statements made by the President and Secretary Stimson. Why, I don't know, unless the prestige of the two high offices demanded especial attention.

In effect, the alleged releases of the Board's Report were not releases of the Reports; they were releases of the President and Secretary of War in defense of General Marshall.

A few days later the morning paper at Columbus carried the headline, *BYRNES RAPS PEARL HARBOR BOARD.*

The new Secretary of State seemed highly offended that Army officers, in the discharge of their official duties, should invade the field of our international relations. Apparently he hadn't gotten completely oriented and did not know of the very great influence which the State Department can have in the conduct of our military and naval men.

It was apparent to me that the President and the Secretary of War had timed the releases of the reports, and had given the information to the Press in such form as to protect General Marshall. They reached the public shortly after the surrender of the Japanese, and the stories stressed the criticisms of the report, and told little of the reports. The United Press sent out the bare conclusions of the Army Board, with no supporting evidence, but Mr. Stimson's criticism was reported in full. This release contained one part report, eight parts criticism.

The first part of the Associated Press report was almost identical with that of the United Press.

Highly intelligent people in different sections of the country have questioned me constantly about Pearl Harbor. Many of the questions have been directed to very material and simple occurrences in the story. This ignorance can be understood, in the light of Washington's successful efforts to conceal the story. Frequently I have been asked to write this history.

I am passing on my recollection of our investigation in the following pages. I have attempted to tell the story as it was developed by the Board. There may be some slight inaccuracies, but the material incidents are here. It is hoped that those who read this story will be able to write conclusions of their own, when the end is reached.

Biography

Henry Dozier Russell was born in Henry County, Georgia, on December 28, 1889. He was the fourth of six children of Henry McDowell Russell and Mary Kelley Russell whose Scots-Irish ancestors had migrated from County Antrim, Ireland, in 1770 through the port of Charleston, South Carolina, first into "upcountry" South Carolina and, a generation later, into northern Georgia after it was opened to settlers in 1825 through treaty with the Creek Indians.

He received his A. B. degree from the University of Georgia in 1912, having been elected to Phi Beta Kappa, and was graduated with first honor from the University of Georgia Law School in 1914. His participation in R.O.T.C. seems not to have sparked any particular interest in military matters and he began to practice law in Jackson, Georgia, in association with Ernest M. Smith of McDonough. In 1916 he was asked to take charge of the Jackson Rifles, a unit of the National Guard. The newly commissioned captain was soon sent, with his unit, to the Mexican border under the command of General John J. Pershing following the Pancho Villa raids. World War I followed quickly and he attained the rank of major while serving in France as Provost Marshal for all American troops in the Paris sector. It was during World War I that he began to form his firmly held belief that the military should always be controlled by civilians and that the civilian soldier was at least as competent as the career soldier.

Returning to civilian life, he practiced law in Macon, Georgia, with friends from university days in the firm they created as Brock, Sparks, and Russell. In 1922 he married Carolyn Crawley from Madison, Georgia, whom he had known since their days in Jackson where she had taught elocution and directed recreation. They had no children. He served as city attorney in 1924-25. During the Great Depression in the early 1930s, the law school friends went separate ways and "Dick" Russell, a nickname acquired at the university, joined the firm of Harris, Harris, Russell, and Weaver.

His interest in military matters continued to develop through the National Guard in the lean years of disarmament between 1920 and 1940. In 1922 he organized the 59th Infantry Brigade and was its commander until 1932 when he was made commander of the 30th Infantry "Old Hickory" Division. When the National Guard was mobilized in September of 1940, fifteen months before the Japanese attack on Pearl Harbor, Major General Russell led troops from four states into training at Fort Jackson, South Carolina, a few miles from the place where his immigrant ancestors had settled 170 years earlier. By 1942 many National Guard leaders had been retired or reassigned to make room for Regular Army leadership. General Russell was relieved of his command shortly before the 30th Division was sent overseas. His account of these experiences was privately published soon after the war under the title, "The Purge of the 30th Division."

He served for the remainder of World War II as a member of the War Department Manpower Board stationed in Columbus, Ohio, interrupted only by his assignment to the Army's Pearl Harbor Investigation Board from July to October 1944. He sought vigorously to be relieved of that assignment but was told that his selection had been dictated by the desire of the War Department to have a lawyer with military background on the Board. This may have been a stipulation of Secretary of War Henry L. Stimson who was himself a lawyer with military experience in World War I. Russell's recollection of his experiences on the Pearl Harbor Board was dictated in January 1946, only fifteen months after the conclusion of the investigation.

The two World War II experiences that he wrote about—the displacement of National Guard officers and the Pearl Harbor investigation—confirmed his formative World War I perception of contempt on the part of the career military for the traditional civilian soldiers of a democracy. Throughout his life he continued to question the professional military establishment which he considered too "Prussian" in style, philosophy, and fraternalism. He must have been heartened by reports after the war that the War Department had selected his old unit, the 30th Division, as the best of the Army in

France in World War II. The selection committee reportedly cited the exceptional treatment of enlisted men by line officers, most of whom had been trained by General Russell.

Until his retirement from the National Guard in 1951 with the rank of Lieutenant General, he was busy participating in Guard reorganization, shouldering a greater share of the law practice his partners had held together during the war years, and debating publicly and privately the issues of the day. He was active in various organizations associated with the practice of law and with the military. He was an ordained deacon in the Presbyterian Church. His beloved wife died in 1958. The National Guard Armory in Macon was named for him in 1961. He won a $2.5 million tax judgment, one of the largest ever at that time, for a client. He continued to practice law with Harris, Russell, and Watkins until overtaken by a stroke. He died on December 31, 1972.

In a two-column news story published Janaury 2, 1973, more than 27 years after the end of World War II, *The New York Times* noted his death and observed that the Army's Pearl Harbor Report was "severely critical of everyone from Secretary of State Cordell Hull to Gen. George C. Marshall, Army Chief of Staff, for their roles in the Pearl Harbor disaster."

Although interest may be more widespread in the dictated recollection of his experiences as a member of the Army Pearl Harbor Investigation Board, his own passion was for the deeper issue of military leadership style appropriate for a democracy. He opposed universal military training and peacetime conscription as antithetical to the body politic. The question with which he wrestled is one that continues in various forms for every would-be democracy: What kind of military?

1 | The Board

The Army Pearl Harbor Board was appointed pursuant to the provision of a public law enacted by the Congress. This law was approved by the President on June 13, 1944. Unlike the Roberts Commission, which came into being by executive order, the Board was appointed by the Secretary of War under the direction of Congress. The designation of the members of the Board was the sole function of the War Department in connection with its existence. This origin gave to the Board an independence of action that might have been lacking under other conditions.

The order creating the Board and defining its mission provided, "Pursuant to the provisions of Public Law 339, 78th Congress, approved 13 June, 1944, a board of officers is hereby appointed to ascertain and report the facts relating to the attack made by the Japanese Armed Forces upon the territory of Hawaii on 7 December, 1941, and to make such recommendations as it may deem proper."

Following this recital, the order then named the members of the Board as follows:

Lt. General George Grunert,
Major General Henry D. Russell,
Major General Walter H. Frank
Colonel Charles W. West (Recorder without vote)

Later Colonel Harry A. Toulmin was named as the executive officer of the Board, and Major Henry C. Clausen was designated for duty with the Board, as assistant recorder.

The order provided further that military and civilian personnel would render the Board all necessary information and assistance. The

Board could request military and civilian personnel to be assigned to aid in the accomplishment of the mission.

The order gave the Board very broad powers. The mission assigned was limited and clear. The Board was to ascertain and report the facts relating to the Pearl Harbor attack, and make such recommendations as it might deem proper. The Board construed this language in connection with the Public Law already referred to. Paragraph 2 of that law stated:

> The Secretary of War and the Secretary of the Navy are severally directed to proceed forthwith with an investigation into the facts surrounding the catastrophe described in Section 1 above (the Pearl Harbor disaster) and to commence such proceedings against such persons as the facts may justify.

Thus construed, the Board conceived it to be its duty to examine all material facts relating to the attack, and evaluate such facts to determine if disciplinary action against any person or persons in the Army of the United States was justified. Early in its deliberations the Board fixed its missions in line with the provisions of the law and the War Department order. Primarily, it was interested in the conduct of Army personnel. Secondarily, it would examine the conduct of all other governmental agencies or persons to the end that all who influenced Army personnel might be known. In this latter category were the President, the Secretary of State and the Navy. The Board was not concerned with derelictions of the Navy or the decisions and conduct of the State Department or the President, unless such derelictions and conduct had its bearing on Army operations. A clear understanding of the limitations imposed on the Army Pearl Harbor Board, by the law and order creating it, is essential to a proper consideration of this story.

The Personnel of the Board

In the preface, attention has been called to the attacks on the conclusions of the Board. Personal friends sent me a copy of the column Merry-Go-Round, which is written by the well-known columnist and commentator, Drew Pearson. This story appeared throughout the country under date of September 12, 1945. The following is the quotation to which attention is invited:

> Some military observers see significance in the makeup of the Army's Pearl Harbor Board and the fact that it criticized Chief of Staff General Marshall. One member was Maj. Gen. Henry Russell of Macon, Ga., who commanded the Thirtieth Division made up of Georgia National Guardsmen at Fort Jackson, S. C., from September 1940, to May 1942. Then just as the division was about to go overseas, he was relieved—This was in line with the Army's frequently unfair policy of taking commands away from National Guard officers in favor of West Pointers and regulars—General Russell resented this bitterly. He had spent almost 20 years with the Georgia National Guard and had a fine overseas record in the last war.
>
> So he protested right up to General Marshall himself. Marshall, however, refused to change the order. Russell stayed home and eventually became a member of the Pearl Harbor Board where he helped find Marshall guilty of neglect....Gen. George Grunert, who headed the Pearl Harbor inquiry, an A-1 officer, is another who had trouble at the top. Serving in the Philippines under MacArthur along with Lieut. Col. Dwight Eisenhower, both he and Eisenhower got in wrong with MacArthur and were sent home. It was the best break Eisenhower ever had...Grunert enlisted as a private, never went to West Point.

This printed story quoting "some military observers" is a direct challenge to the good faith of two members of the Board, General

Grunert and myself. "Some military observers" charged that General Grunert and I had acted in a spirit of revenge.

Such comments attacking the good faith of the Board requires a brief statement about the members of the Board and their past histories.

Lt. Gen. George Grunert

The order appointing the Board designated Lt. Gen. George Grunert as the President. As a lieutenant general he was the senior member of the Board. His decisions on administrative matters were final. In the field of investigation and decision all of the members of the Board participated on equal terms.

General Grunert was a typical professional soldier. He was commissioned from the ranks and by hard and conscientious work had become a lieutenant general and was at the time of his service on the Board in command of the Eastern Defense Command. Born in 1880, he was rapidly approaching the retirement age of 64, when appointed as the President of the Board. I regarded him as a member of the Marshall Party in the Army. Those connected with the Board reached the conclusion that he was a great favorite in the War Department. He had served on the General Staff and was thoroughly indoctrinated with its cautious procedure. Particularly did this General Staff training reflect itself in General Grunert's approach to the preparation of the report. He was very fond of such expressions as "it appears", which is so characteristic of the reserve manifested by the typical officer with general staff training.

Just prior to the outbreak of war with Japan, General Grunert was in command of the Philippine Department. He was succeeded in that command by General MacArthur. His service in the Orient gave him a background which proved very valuable in our investigation.

He brought to the Board certain well-fixed views. He believed that General Short had been assigned a mission at Pearl Harbor and had been given certain means for its accomplishment. Short did not employ the means, which were available to him for the defense of the Navy at Pearl Harbor and the Army installations on the Island of

Oahu; hence he failed in his mission and must bear the consequences. Insofar as the investigation related to General Short, this
thinking of General Grunert was final. At no time during the investigation did he vary from it in the smallest detail.

The second of his fixed views grew out of his great desire to
vindicate the War Department. It was perfectly evident from the very
beginning that he would make every effort to compile a record that
would free the War Department from any dereliction of duty in
connection with the attack at Pearl Harbor. His obstinacy and this
determination served at times as a hindrance to the investigation.

As evidence came in, pointing clearly to failures in the War
Department, he retreated in a measure from his first position. He
was willing to find that certain staff officers in the War Department
were guilty of dereliction of duty to the extent of downright
inefficiency, but he continued to defend vigorously the Chief of
Staff, Marshall. In this defense of Marshall he employed everything at
his command: argument, persuasion and finally attempted coercion.
For some reason, which is not clear to me, he signed the report as
prepared. He also participated in the preparation of the report.

In the article of Mr. Drew Pearson, quoted from above, he refers
to the fact that General Grunert had not fared too well with the high
command in Washington, implying that General Grunert had taken
advantage of his opportunity as a member of the Army Pearl Harbor
Board to even scores with those whom he regarded as the authors of
his relief from the command of the Philippine Department. It is difficult to conceive how so great a mistake could be made by anyone.
The "military observers" who supplied the information for Mr. Pearson about General Grunert and his attitude toward Marshall showed
an amazing ignorance of actual conditions.

Nothing said about General Grunert must be construed to mean
that he limited in any way the scope of the investigation. With one
possible exception, which will be noted later, he was in complete
accord with the Board's policy of investigating any and everything
that might have any bearing on the Pearl Harbor defeat. Repeatedly
he asked witnesses if they knew anything about which they had not
testified that might be of help to the Board in discovering the full
truth. It was only in attempting to develop the testimony in support

of his fixed ideas that he manifested his desires as to the Board's findings. In all fairness to General Grunert, it should be said that this approach could have been activated by the very highest motive and based on what he considered as sound reasoning.

Major General Walter H. Frank

General Frank was a graduate of West Point. He was the only member of the Board who was educated at that institution.

To me, General Frank was one of the most unusual personalities I have ever met. Notwithstanding his West Point training and his long service in the Army, he was possessed of an independence in thinking and action wholly unexpected, if not amazing.

He came to the Board with one fixed opinion. He maintained that idea throughout the investigation, never wavering from it for one moment. In substance, he believed that such information as was possessed by General Short at the time of the Pearl Harbor attack was sufficient to indicate to General Short that some aggressive action by the Japanese might be expected. General Short did not act on the principle that required that he anticipate the worst that the Japanese could do to him and prepare to meet it. The violation of this principle was a dereliction of duty, for which General Short must suffer. All of his questioning of General Short was influenced if not dominated, by this one thought.

Other than this conception, General Frank approached the investigation of the disaster with a perfectly open mind. He was seeking the truth and was not interested in its effect on anyone's fortunes.

This independence of thinking on the part of General Frank, although his superiors might have been involved, was wholly unexpected and most gratifying.

Before leaving this description of Generals Grunert and Frank, it should be said that they labored on this Board under circumstances which were most trying and required a high degree of courage. Both were serving in grades much higher than those that they hold on the permanent Army list. They were purely temporary in nature and were being enjoyed through the sufferance of the Chief of Staff of the Army. A one-sentence order could reduce them to their permanent ranks. Both were completing long military careers. So far as I know, neither had anything adverse in his military record. I sympathized with them deeply in the problem that they faced.

Major General Henry D. Russell

Were it not for the attacks which have been made on the report and members of the Board, including myself, I would not write the following.

As stated in the preface, I wanted no part of the Pearl Harbor investigation. General Short had been my first and most efficient corps commander during World War II. He came to Columbia, S. C., in the fall of 1940 as the Commanding General of the First Army Corps. The 30th Division of National Guard troops was assigned to that corps. I was commanding the 30th Division.

General Short approached the Division with the usual Regular Army prejudice toward the National Guard. He and I differed from the very beginning on some questions of major policies. It was his desire that I replace senior National Guard officers with Regular Army officers who had been attached to the Division at the date of its mobilization. Further, he wanted me to bring into the Division numerous graduates of R. O. T. C. institutions to increase the commissioned personnel of the Division to war strength. I refused to fire the National Guard officers to make way for the regulars. Similarly, I insisted that the non-commissioned officers of the Division who were perfectly capable of serving as commissioned officers be promoted, and R. O. T. C. graduates be used for deficiency numbers only.

General Short was very persistent in his demands, and when he was ordered to the Hawaiian Department in late December 1940, he was pressing for the accomplishment of his desires. Notwithstanding these disagreements and some others, I gained a very fine impression of him both as an officer and as a man. Remarks that he made about me in Columbia, S. C., and later in Washington, D. C., indicated that he felt about me much as I felt about him. In all events, when, in retrospect, I compare General Short with the others who came after him, such as General Lear and General Thompson, I realize that Short was an officer of outstanding character and ability.

I knew little about the Pearl Harbor attack. I had read the Roberts Report, superficially, and was somewhat surprised to find that it charged Short with dereliction of duty, which embraced a lack of alertness. Others in the chain of command had been exonerated by the Roberts Commission. This report was accepted by me as being accurate in every respect. Therefore, I dismissed the entire subject with the remark that the very best of men some times are caught off-guard.

Insofar as I had any views at all about the nature and scope of the investigation, I believed that the principal mission of the Board was to determine whether or not Short's derelictions of duty were such as to justify a trial by courts-martial. Every judge and juror who has been called upon to inquire into the conduct of a friend for the purpose of determining whether such friend should be punished will appreciate the feeling with which I approached this investigation of General Short's conduct. It was one of those unpleasant duties that must be done.

It did not occur to me that the investigation would reveal facts that might reflect most seriously on the efficiency of the War Department, and the Chief of Staff, General Marshall. Had I known of the coming developments, I would have pressed, with much more vigor, my request to be relieved from service on the Board.

I had entered the military service in September 1940 in command of one of the first four National Guard divisions to be mobilized. I was in command of that division until the first day of May 1942, at which time I was relieved from the command of the Division and sent before a reclassification board. This service was under conditions almost intolerable in their nature. Such conditions were created by the Regular Army as a part of an over-all policy to eliminate the National Guard as a major component of the Army of the United States.

It was my firm belief that the Chief of Staff Marshall played a large, if not determining part, in the formulation and execution of this anti-National Guard policy. Certain it is that his conduct in the purge of the 30th Division was utterly and almost unbelievably reprehensible. That story is entirely too long to be told here. It will be told elsewhere and at a later time.

I realize full well that the average professional soldier cannot conceive of my approaching an investigation of any matter in which General Marshall was involved with an open mind. Nevertheless, the members of my civilian profession of lawyers and judges, I am sure, will agree with me when I say that an investigation under such conditions had the very opposite tendency and drives one to view all facts developed with the very greatest caution to the end that an injustice may not be done or conclusions reached as the result of personal likes or dislikes.

The attitude of "some military observers" of Mr. Pearson's column is not difficult to understand, when the thinking of the typical Regular Army officer is known.

2 | Preliminaries

The first meeting of the Board was held in the Pentagon Building on the 20th day of July, 1944. It was an organizational meeting where many administrative details were discussed. At this meeting General Grunert told the Board that he had just finished a conference with General McNarney, who, at the time was Deputy Chief of Staff and serving immediately under General Marshall. General Grunert had submitted to General McNarney questions seeking information about the investigation. General McNarney had answered all of these questions, and in the main such answers were regarded by me as being entirely fair to the Board, and manifesting a serious desire on the part of the War Department to help the Board. We were given authority to deal directly with all agencies of the War Department in Washington. This eliminated the necessity of sending requests for information through channels. All officers in the War Department would be instructed to give the Board every assistance. It is important to bear this in mind when our relations with G-2 of the War Department are discussed hereafter.

All Army personnel, wherever located, were made available to the Board as witnesses, with one exception, to wit: Commanders in theatres of operations could appear before the Board only with the approval of their superiors.

This limitation had no practical effect on the investigation as all officers requested appeared before the Board, irrespective of where they were or what they were doing.

General McNarney had told General Grunert that the Navy would work in full harmony with us. We were not permitted to deal directly with the Navy or the State Department. Our requests were to be sent through channels, which meant that we would send them to the Secretary of War, who would forward such of them as he approved to the interested departments. This procedure worked very smoothly throughout the entire investigation. Insofar as I recall, the Navy denied only one request, the others none.

Informal discussions were had between the members of the Navy Board investigating Pearl Harbor, and the Army Board, relating to purely administrative details.

At the initial meeting of the Board General Grunert stated that the War Department had fixed October 14 as the date when the investigation should be completed and the report finished and submitted. It was my impression then and is now that the reason for the selection of this date was entirely political. The Presidential election would occur in early November. The War Department did not want to be charged with delaying the submission of its Pearl Harbor Report to influence the approaching election. When the announcement of this time limitation was made I regarded the decision as very unfortunate. I thought the Board should be unlimited in the scope of its investigation and the time required for its work. The great confusion in the minds of the people of America about Pearl Harbor and the necessity for clarification demanded that the Board do a thorough job. I regarded political implications of the Pearl Harbor disaster as unimportant. I doubt that this limitation affected the Board's findings in any way, or prevented it from completing its work in every detail. It was necessary to proceed without delay and to work continuously. The Board, realizing the necessity for such continuous work, went about it so as to finish the job by the named date.

Preliminary Research

A few days were spent in reading available records. In the main they consisted of the Roberts Report, including the evidence introduced before the Roberts Commission, together with records from the Office of the Adjutant General which had been procured by the Recorder, Colonel West.

One striking incident of this period was the submission to the Board by Major Clausen of a very complete copy of charges and specifications that had been prepared against General Short. The history of these charges and specifications, insofar as I know it, is about as follows: The Judge Advocate's office had been directed by the War Department to prepare charges and specifications upon which General Short could be tried. They were complete and extensive. A charge would be made and, immediately following it, specifications would be set forth in support of the charge. Many of the specifications were based on the evidence developed by the Roberts Commission. Reference to the pages of the Roberts Report would follow the specification. This enabled the members of the Pearl Harbor Board to review the Roberts Report with such guidance as these charges and specifications supplied.

The charges and specifications had been carefully prepared and alleged an extremely strong case against General Short. They were perfect. As a matter of fact, their great perfection attracted attention. The derelictions charged against General Short were so serious in their nature that it was impossible to understand why General Short had not been tried on them long before.

Probably because of my training as a lawyer in civil life, I read these charges and specifications with great caution. Their form and substance had all the earmarks of the experienced prosecutor. I followed two or three of the more important and impressive charges through, analyzing carefully the supporting evidence. Any suspicions that I might have had about the nature of these charges and specifications were fully justified by this limited investigation. It was very clear that isolated sentences had been selected from the Roberts record in support of charges and specifications that could not have been sustained by an intelligent study of the Roberts record, as a whole.

Notwithstanding that we later learned these charges and specifications were absolutely unsound and could not have been supported, they were very helpful to us, as a background for the investigation. Our study of the Roberts report was likewise of great assistance. The evidence which that Commission had taken was voluminous, containing much that was material and much that was immaterial. This is not said in a spirit of criticism. Conditions under which the Roberts investigation was made were such as to result in exploring much that had no bearing on the causes of the Pearl Harbor disaster. The Army Pearl Harbor Board was faced with the same situation. There is a great deal of evidence in the record developed by the Board that is immaterial.

It is my belief that we should have spent a longer period in our general investigation and planning. Such procedure would doubtless have resulted in our selecting the material and discarding the immaterial.

During the preparatory phase of our work the War Department submitted to the Board a letter from General Short in which he requested that he be permitted to attend the Board's hearing. It was his desire to be accompanied by his attorney, a General Green. This request was considered and a decision was reached to deny it.

My reasoning was that the Board had been appointed to make an investigation to determine whether or not any one should be subjected to disciplinary measures because of the attack at Pearl Harbor—not to try General Short. It was the duty of the Board to approach this investigation with an open mind and to take all steps necessary to develop a complete history of the attack. Evidence favorable to General Short or any one else should be developed to the extent that evidence unfavorable to Short or such officer might be developed. I believed that if General Short and his counsel appeared before the Board we would soon have a trial of the issues in which Short, and his counsel, would be appearing as the defendant, opposed by the lawyers who had been assigned to the Board. Freedom of the Board, under these circumstances, to participate in the investigation would be limited to a damaging extent.

We made available to General Short all of the evidence as rapidly as it came into the record. We told him that he would be given full opportunity to rebut, in any way he desired, anything that might be in the record. The fact that General Short made only a very brief statement when recalled at the end of the investigation, is, to my mind, evidence of the fairness of the Board's work.

In retrospect and in the light of subsequent developments, I doubt the wisdom of our decision to exclude Short and his counsel from the proceedings. In the description of the attitude of the members of the Board at the outset of the investigation, the fixed

views of Generals Grunert and Frank were recited. It became
apparent soon after the hearings began that neither Grunert nor
Frank was interested in evidence favorable to General Short. On the
contrary, they had condemned him already and apparently could see
no good purpose to be served by placing such evidence in the
record. I had no feeling about it and unfortunately found myself
alone in my efforts to develop facts favorable to Short.

In this preliminary period, General Grunert referred to our relations with the President, the War Department, the Navy Department
and the State Department. He seemed concerned about the Board's
investigation of the President and these other agencies of the government. It was at this time that our decision touching these matters
was made.

I was outspoken in defining my position. Our mission was limited
to military personnel for recommendations, but not thus prescribed
for the investigation. To state it another way, the acts of anyone,
including the President, whose official position authorized or
required action on matters affecting the disaster, were the subject of
investigation and should be closely scrutinized by the Board to the
end that proper conclusions as to the cause of the disaster might be
reached. This was the Board's policy.

General Grunert divided the work, assigning to each member of
the Board certain phases of the investigation. He made it clear that
the responsibility for developing the evidence in the several fields
would be with the member of the Board to whom such fields were
assigned, but emphasized that each member of the Board must
maintain his interest in the entire investigation. In this assignment,
General Grunert was to be primarily concerned with the investigation of the Navy and the operations at Pearl Harbor. General Frank
was to investigate the Wyman-Rohl affair and develop the operations
of the air corps in connection with the defense of Pearl Harbor. I
was given the War Department, and later, as a corollary to the work
of the War Department, I was assigned the duty of a study of the
records at Pearl Harbor, and the relation of the State Department
and the President to the defeat at Pearl Harbor.

General Grunert announced that hearings would begin at a fixed
and early date. The first witnesses to be called were from the War

Department. The War Department documents must be ready when the hearings began. This decision was unfortunate. The conduct of the War Department became the major part of the investigation. A great deal more time for preliminary investigation should have been made available. Nevertheless, I worked hurriedly and I believe developed all of the information possible, when the attitude of the War Department toward the investigation is considered.

I don't know what impression the other members of the Board had after our preliminary investigation. I had a distinct feeling that much which was material to a complete understanding of the history of the Pearl Harbor attack was missing from the records. This feeling was confirmed and strengthened by the developments of the immediate future.

3 | The War Department

The War Department and the Hawaiian Department were the agencies of the Army responsible for the conduct of Army forces at Pearl Harbor. There were no intervening headquarters. Orders were issued from the War Department to the Hawaiian Department directly. Under military law and procedure the head of the War Department, to wit, the Chief of Staff of the Army, and Commanding General of the Hawaiian Department were the responsible officers. Expressed in terms of personalities, General Marshall in Washington and General Short in Hawaii were the two men responsible to the American people for the efficient employment of the army forces on the Island of Oahu. This is the inexorable law of our military establishment. It applies to those in all ranks and echelons of command. It applied to Marshall and Short. None is too big and none is too small to escape its effect. All the efforts to shield Marshall from this rule of law are ludicrous to military men.

My knowledge of the War Department and its operations was the result of discussion with numerous officers who at one time or another had been in the War Department and on the General Staff. I had never served in the War Department or on the General Staff.

As stated before, it was my impression that the records which had been read during the preliminary phase of our investigation were not a complete history of those facts and things which might throw light on our disastrous defeat at Pearl Harbor. When General Grunert assigned me to explore the War Department's relation to the Pearl Harbor history, I knew that it was my job to develop such facts as had not been disclosed to us. The great weakness in the records, as seen by us, was the astounding lack of information about the movement of the Japanese task force that struck at Pearl Harbor. It was difficult for me to reconcile this condition with intelligent and mildly efficient operations of the military intelligence division of the General Staff, which is a part of the office of G-2.

It was impossible not to contrast this apparent lack of knowledge on the part of our military and naval intelligence with the very great familiarity that the Japanese had of the situation at Pearl Harbor. This familiarity was reflected in the description of the attack on December 7, 1941, contained in a written statement submitted to the Roberts Commission by General Short. In this written statement Short referred to the splendid planning of the Japanese task force. Targets had been assigned to such forces with definiteness and preciseness. Planes and guns especially adapted to different missions were sent to the attack in such manner as to indicate clearly that the Japanese high command knew the location of our installations and what we had in each of them.

In hurriedly outlining a plan for the investigation of the War Department, I was partially informed. Some months prior to my assignment to the Army Pearl Harbor Board I had read Mr. Walter Lippmann's book, *U. S. Foreign Policy: Shield of the Republic.* In that book appeared the very striking statement that we were in the War because the Japanese had refused to withdraw from Indo-China. He cited as his authority for this statement the book which had been published by the State Department, *Peace and War, United States Foreign Policy, 1931-1941.*

I was very much interested by Mr. Lippmann's statement, but skeptical that the State Department had published any book, the contents of which would justify a conclusion that we went to War to get the Japanese out of Indo-China. I recall very well that, when I read Mr. Lippmann's statement, I remarked to someone in my office, "It will be most difficult hereafter to explain to the families of deceased and disabled soldiers that their boys went to death or to a life of disability to get the Japanese Army out of Indo-China."

After some effort, I secured a copy of *Peace and War* and read Mr. Lippman's reference. He had cited the telegram of December 6 sent by President Roosevelt to Emperor Hirohito. At the end of this telegram the following sentence appeared: "Thus a withdrawal of the Japanese forces from Indo-China would result in the assurance of peace throughout the whole of the South Pacific."

We will not discuss further, at this time, the details of our negotiations with the Japanese. They will be set forth in a later chapter that deals with the State Department and the President.

I had studied carefully the State Department book *Peace and War*. The pattern of our negotiations with Japan and their trend was clear-cut and unmistakable. The relations in 1941 were becoming increasingly tense. War was inevitable and imminent. There were proposals and counter-proposals, threats and counter-threats. Irreconcilable disagreements were through all of the pages of the book. If the nature of these negotiations was being transmitted to Short in Hawaii, he should have been deeply impressed with the gravity of the situation and the necessity for the very greatest caution in his major mission of protecting the Navy. After reading this book it was difficult then for me to understand how the Japanese accomplished the complete surprise which characterized their attack at Pearl Harbor. I thought that the War and Navy Departments had not been told by the State Department of the growing tenseness in our relations with Japan.

After my selection by General Grunert for the investigation of the War Department, I returned to the records of the Roberts Commission. There I read the testimony of such War Department witnesses as had appeared before that Commission. My chief interest centered in the testimony of General Marshall, as the responsible head of the War Department. To my disappointment I discovered that such testimony as he gave had been omitted from the record. There was a brief statement that General Marshall had appeared before the Board and had described certain operations of the War Department; that these operations were of such secret nature that the Commission had felt justified in omitting them from its record. I must admit that I read this with some suspicions. General Marshall's technique in his appearance before public boards, particularly Congressional committees, was well known to me, and I have heard others refer to it. In advance he acquaints himself with what such bodies may desire and determines what he is willing to tell them. When he appears before the group, he immediately launches into a discussion of the subject and relies on his great powers of salesmanship to overwhelm the body to which he is talking. Ordinarily when he has finished with his discussion those to whom he was talking are overcome and excuse him. For the lack of a better term, we might describe this technique as the "Congressional Brush-off."

The War Department Organization

A brief description of the General Staff on December 7, 1941 is essential to a clear understanding of the plan for developing the relation of the War Department to Pearl Harbor. Marshall was Chief of Staff. Associated with him and under his immediate supervision and control were the sections of the General Staff. They corresponded roughly to the staff sections of any high command throughout the Army. Those staff sections important to the investigation were the Military Intelligence Division of G-2 and the War Plans Division, which is a part of the Operations Division. The War Plans Division is a relatively recent growth in our staff organization at Washington.

Source of Evidence. In addition to such records and evidence as were available to the Board from the report of the Roberts Commission, it could broaden the scope of the investigation, by a further search of records in the War Department, and by calling officers who were on duty in the interested sections of the General Staff on December 7, 1941.

The Records. I spent several days in my search of War Department records. In preparation for this search, I talked to officers from the Third Section of the General Staff, officers from the War Plans Division, officers from the office of G-2, and finally with representatives of the Adjutant General's office. In these conferences I learned that the records in which we were interested if any existed, could be found either in the office of the Adjutant General, or in the office of G-2. The War Plans Division filed all its documents with the Adjutant General.

Too much cannot be said for the cooperation given by Colonel Sepulvada and his associates in the office of the Adjutant General. They were furnished with a memorandum in which we described the documents desired. The Board wanted to know the extent to which Short was supervised by the War Department; the instructions that had been issued to Short; interference, if any, with Short in his training of his troops, and in the administration of his affairs in the Hawaiian Department. We requested documents touching these same matters prior to the time that Short reached the Hawaiian Department, which might have been in effect when Short took over. We discovered very little. Apparently the Adjutant General had combed his files for the Roberts Commission and had delivered the things that he considered relevant and material to Colonel West, the Board's recorder. Nevertheless, I spent possibly a day and a half reading documents that had been selected for me in response to the Board's memorandum. Of all of these documents I can recall only one that I considered important. It covered an all-out alert which had been ordered in the Hawaiian Department in July 1940 and prior to the time that Short had been made the Commanding General at Hawaii.

The record established conclusively that the War Department had not interfered with General Short in his administration of the Hawaiian Department, or in his training of his troops. The War Department announced broad policies for the direction of the Commanding General of the Hawaiian Department and left to him the methods for the execution of such policies. So long as the planning and execution of the Commanding General of the Hawaiian Department were in harmony with War Department policies he was not disturbed. It was only when such planning and execution by the Commanding General of the Hawaiian Department conflicted with such War Department policies that the War Department intervened. We never discovered anything in the relations between General Marshall and Short which Short could have construed as interference. There was a spirit of helpfulness and understanding.

The War Department and the Hawaiian Department were in complete harmony as to the mission of the Army at Pearl Harbor.

Both Marshall and Short testified that the protection of the Navy was its only mission.

G-2 Documents. Before analyzing such data as was contained in the written records obtained from the office of the Adjutant General, it might be well to discuss our experiences with the Office of Military Intelligence. I had expected to find in this office information of the most vital character. It was here that all of the data about the plans of the Japanese should have been filed. The Board was investigating the Pearl Harbor attack to discover Army derelictions, if any existed. The element of surprise was the military crime to be investigated. Alertness to have prevented this surprise was the function of G-2. We were very anxious to determine what the War Department knew, if anything, that it did not transmit to Short. The very first step in the investigation was to learn all that G-2 knew. Our relations with G-2, in the investigation, were just as unsatisfactory as our relations with the Adjutant General had been satisfactory. In response to our request, a Colonel Clark came to the Board's office in the Munitions Building. As I remember, he was accompanied by Brig. Gen. Osmun. These two officers were in charge of the Military Intelligence Division of G-2. I remember Clark very well. He was the spokesman. He had reached the Army through the Academy at West Point, having been sent there by Senator Barkley from Kentucky. To refer to Clark as explosive and garrulous is something of an understatement. He came to the Board's office early in the investigation and before memoranda requesting G-2 information had been put in final form. Some notes had been written on scratch paper by me. Before Clark left the office, I had one of the stenographers transcribe these notes and handed Clark a copy. We asked to be furnished all information in the possession of G-2 from which deductions were made as to the intentions and plans of the Japanese. We also requested a copy of all information about this same subject that had been transmitted to Short in the Hawaiian Department. We specified G-2 reports and similar documents, and then so phrased our request as to include all of that type of data and information commonly in the possession of G-2 sections throughout the Army. I was very careful to make this memorandum all inclusive.

Shortly thereafter Colonel Clark returned to our office and announced that he had completed his search of the records of G-2. He had discovered nothing. He then launched into a very vigorous criticism of military intelligence. His deluge of words lasted for some time. I recall quite vividly his statement that in pre-war days the chief function of G-2 was to get the picture of the Commanding General's wife in the papers. When Clark had left the office and I had recovered, I became very suspicious of the treatment that the Board was receiving from G-2. Clark was only a colonel. Notwithstanding that fact, he was most caustic in his criticism of the entire military intelligence set-up of the Army. By implication, this involved many of his superiors. I could not believe that Clark was speaking so vigorously without the knowledge, consent or approval of someone higher in authority. Even a Kentucky colonel with Senator Barkely's backing would not have been so bold.

Was he playing a game with me? So strong were my suspicions about it that I acted upon the theory. I planned a game of my own. The basic thought of this game on my part was a vigorous criticism of the office of G-2 in Washington. I continued this criticism in my contacts with the office of G-2 in the Hawaiian Department.

In discussing the failure of G-2 to function, both Osmun and Clark, and later General Miles who was G-2 at the time of the attack at Pearl Harbor, had complained a great deal of the lack of support for their section. They stated that Congress had been very parsimonious in its appropriation of funds to carry on intelligence work throughout the world. I made a little investigation and discovered that the appropriations to G-2 had grown from about $50,000 in 1935 to approximately $500,000 in 1941. While this latter figure is inconsiderable when compared to the sums supposed to have been expended by Germany and Japan for similar purposes in 1941, it is very evident that there were enough dollars appropriated to purchase a great deal of spying. I recall that when the evidence on these appropriations was introduced General Grunert became excited and wanted to know if I was not going to prove for what G-2 spent this money. He apparently did not realize that I was attempting to smoke out information, which was probably being concealed from us.

Another complaint registered by Generals Miles and Osmun and Colonel Clark, was that G-2 had been discriminated against in the assignment of officers. They stated that the bright officers who finished the schools were all interested in becoming field marshals, hence were not interested in G-2 work. I regarded both Osmun and Clark as much more capable than the average professional army officers I knew.

In these efforts to force a disclosure of G-2 information, I was armed with an argument that was unanswerable and doubtless proved very embarrassing to interested officers. I constantly referred to the size of the Japanese task force that attacked Pearl Harbor. It was not easy to picture a considerable armada assembling in some Japanese port and sailing across the Pacific Ocean thousands of miles to a position near Pearl Harbor without being discovered. As a matter of fact, recently the Secretary of the Japanese Naval Ministry has been quoted as saying that the attack on Pearl Harbor was conducted by planes from four aircraft carriers and that these were protected by three battleships, eight cruisers and 20 destroyers. I invited the attention of these officers from G-2 to the absolute lack of information that we had concerning the whereabouts of the Japanese carriers and other elements of the Japanese Navy. I pictured to them the peaceful assembly of the task force off Pearl Harbor, without our knowing anything about it. It was by the merest accident that we had our first inkling of the presence of this great force before the shells began to fall on Oahu. The reference to this discovery was the radar interception only minutes before the attack began.

I am not certain that my remarks about the operations of G-2 had any effect. They might have.

General Miles was called as a witness. He was pressed for information about the records in the office of G-2, and particularly about reports that had been prepared by that office to send to the Field. His testimony on this point was not entirely clear, but he described, in general terms, studies of probable Japanese actions by G-2.

Thereupon I made renewed efforts to get such material documents for the Board.

As a result of those efforts, Colonel Clark came back to the Munitions Building, bringing to my office several large volumes of printed matter. He represented that they had been selected from the files of G-2. I scanned them rather superficially, but to the extent of discovering that they had no bearing at all on the Pearl Harbor disaster and were not remotely related to the information that I was seeking. I told Colonel Clark that the information in these volumes could be obtained from the Encyclopaedia Britannica. To this he readily agreed. I believe now that this move on the part of Clark was a part and parcel of the cover-up policy adopted by the War Department in its dealing with the Army Pearl Harbor Board.

In summary, I realized that all of the investigation made for the purpose of determining what the War Department knew about Japanese plans and intentions on the 7th of December, 1941, had resulted in absolutely nothing. Further, I was convinced that no agency of the War Department could have been as inefficient and downright stupid as the office of G-2 desired the Army Pearl Harbor Board to believe it to have been.

It has been stated that in my work with the War Department I was left free by the other members of the Board to develop anything that I regarded as important to the investigation, with one exception. This exception related to a possible agreement between the British Government and the American Government for joint action in the Pacific in the event Japanese aggression should reach certain limits. I broached that subject in one of our earlier conferences. General Grunert stated he could see no relation between such an agreement, if one existed, and Short's mission at Pearl Harbor. He believed that this field should be left for someone else to explore.

It was my thought then, which I regard as sound now, that overseas department commanders should have known of such agreement, if one existed.

Written Evidence from the War Department. A great many docu-ments were placed in the record by the Board. With the exception of the decoded Japanese messages, which will be discussed in a later part of this story, I now regard only four documents as important. Three of these came from the office of the Adjutant General. The fourth was the joint statement of Marshall and Stark to the President, dated November 27, 1941.

Let us consider at this time the three messages that came to the Board from the office of the Adjutant General.

The first of the October messages was dated October 18, 1941. It was sent from General Marshall to General Short. To understand its full implications, something of its history is essential. It will be remembered that in October 1941, the Konoye Government at Tokyo fell. The belligerent Tojo came into power. This change in the Japanese Government was of vital concern to us. It was important for us to determine the effect of the change on our relations with Japan.

On the 16th day of October, 1941, the Navy sent a message to Kimmel at Pearl Harbor. In that message the Navy told Kimmel in substance that conditions in the Pacific were very serious. It foretold probable hostilities between Japan and Russia. The following remarkable sentence was in the message:

Since Britain and the United States are held responsible by Japan for her present situation there is also a possibility that Japan may attack these two powers.

Short was given this message by Kimmel. He could have deduced but one conclusion from it: a strong probability of war with Japan in the immediate future.

The records in the office of the Adjutant General showed that this Naval message was studied by interested officers in the War Depart-ment. These officers were in agreement that the Naval message to Kimmel was entirely too strong in depicting probable war with Japan. As a result of this estimate of the situation by the War Depart-ment, a radiogram was sent to Short at Hawaii, which is in the fol-lowing language:

> Following War Department estimate of Japanese situation, for your information tension between the United States and Japan remains strained but no abrupt change in Japanese foreign policy appears imminent.

It was extremely interesting to note that this revised prophecy about our relations with the Japanese had the endorsement of General Marshall, General Miles and General Gerow.

The clear force and effect of this message was to advise Short that the Navy was too optimistic about a Japanese war and that he should not regard the Naval message of the 16th too seriously.

The great materiality of this last message grows out of its probable impact on the thinking of Short and his staff, provided they did any thinking. The Army and Navy were in disagreement. Under the general plan, Short and Kimmel were supposed to exchange information which each received from the War and Navy Departments in Washington. Had the messages sent out by the War and Navy Departments been free from conflict the responsible commanders at Pearl Harbor could have attained unity in their thinking. These messages of October, however, reflect a wide disagreement between the War and Navy Departments in their estimates of the Pacific situation. It followed as a matter of course that if Short and Kimmel both saw the messages just described each would have been impressed by the contents of the message received from his superior headquarters. Kimmel would have looked forward to war. Short was told there would be no change in Japan's foreign policy, hence no war.

The reader should be informed at this point that the War Department's message of October 18 was the last word sent to Short prior to December 7 from the War Department, with the single exception of the message of November 27, 1941, which has become famous or notorious as No. 472. It is true that some sabotage messages were sent out from agencies of the War Department, but these do not affect the accuracy of the above statement. From the 18th of October, 1941, until the attack on December 7, Short received from

Marshall only one message relating to the extremely important question of war with Japan.

It is difficult to understand why Marshall and his defenders attach so much importance to Naval messages sent to Kimmel by the Navy Department and supposedly shown to Short, when the wide disagreement between the War Department and the Navy Department on probable Japanese actions in October is considered. Short was guided by instructions from Marshall, not by messages received by Kimmel from the Navy.

No. 472. On the 27th of November, 1941, Marshall sent Short his final warning and orders. They were contained in message No. 472. We will not discuss that message now for the very good reason that when the Board left Washington for Pearl Harbor, it knew little of the history of the message. I had made efforts to discover the author of the message—why it was prepared and, in brief, to develop all of the facts surrounding its preparation, transmission and subsequent handling. Many facts were discovered but we were met with a very great aversion on the part of witnesses who should have been thoroughly familiar with the message and its history. The following is the message in full:

No. 472. Negotiations with Japanese appear to be terminated to all practical purposes with only the barest possibilities that the Japanese Government might come back and offer to continue. Japanese future action unpredictable but hostile action possible at any moment. If hostilities cannot, repeat cannot, be avoided, the U. S. desires that Japan commit the first overt act. This policy should not, repeat not, be construed as restricting you to a course of action that might jeopardize your defense. Prior to hostile Japanese action, you are directed to undertake such reconnaissance and other measures as you deem necessary but these measures should be carried out so as not, repeat not, to alarm the civil population or disclose intent. Report measures taken. Should hostilities occur, you will carry out task assigned in Rainbow Five

as far as they pertain to Japan. Limit dissemination of this
highly secret information to minimum essential officers.

The message is set forth here as it will be necessary to refer to it
throughout the story, and prior to the time that it will be analyzed
fully.

When I read this message, I regarded it as very weak, and a
masterpiece of confusion. I recall quite clearly General Frank's typical
explosion when he read it. In that explosion he referred to it as "this
do-don't message." The description was so apt that it was generally
referred to as the "Do-don't" message from that time forward.

We all realized the great importance of the instructions to Short
contained in the message and many questions were asked throughout the investigation in an effort to account for its unusual form and
substance. During our questioning of some of the officers, the name
of a Colonel Bundy, who was on duty in the War Plans Division, was
frequently mentioned. He was directly responsible for the operations
of the Japanese section of that division. This colonel had been killed
in an aircraft accident. I was deeply concerned over the prospect of
having the preparation of No. 472 placed at the door of this
deceased colonel.

Short's Sabotage Reply. The third document was Short's reply to
Marshall's message. It was brief and clear:

Report Department alerted to prevent sabotage liaison with
Navy REUARD 472 November 27.

This reply of Short's will be discussed in a later part of this story
where 472 is analyzed. It is sufficient to say here that Short's reply
destroyed much of the importance of 472 insofar as these two
messages are related to or affect the dereliction of duty properly
chargeable to Marshall and Short. Despite all of the discussions
about Short's reply, it is overwhelmingly apparent that Short told
Marshall of the condition of readiness of the Army troops in the
Hawaiian Department. Marshall did nothing about it. This by

necessary implication was an approval of Short's decision. So it is that when the exchanges between Marshall and Short are considered, in their entirety, there is an inescapable conclusion that on the 27th day of November Marshall and Short got into the same sabotage bed together.

The Joint Statement. When General Marshall was being questioned about his relations with Short, he read to the Board a statement signed by him and Admiral Stark, Chief of Naval Operations at the time. It was dated November 27, 1941. In the main this statement discussed the state of preparations for war in the Pacific. It recited that every effort was being made to get men and material into the Philippines. It urged delay in bringing on war with Japan to the end that all opportunities for strengthening our forces in the Pacific should be given to our military and naval authorities. It recited details of troop movements in that area.

To me the most significant part of this joint statement was contained in the first two or three sentences. The contents of these sentences are being recited from memory. The language in this statement probably will vary a little from the language in this story. The document began with a sentence to the effect that if current negotiations with Japan fail, indicating uncertainty about this in the minds of Marshall and Stark on November 27, 1941. This expression is followed by the much more important one that the British, Dutch and American representatives conferring together have agreed that "counter-military measures" (I believe that I am quoting the exact words) should not be taken unless and until Japan's forces advanced to or beyond a certain line. This line was defined as being west of 100^0 east and south of 10^0 north. Interpreted, it meant by implication that counter-military measures were recommended when and if the Japanese went too far south or west. In discussing this, General Marshall testified that it was the intent of the three governments to deny the China Sea to the Japanese. I was intensely interested in this agreement and wanted to know if Short knew about it. He did not. Marshall was later asked in writing the direct question, "Who had authority to bind the American Government to take counter-military measures against Japan when her troops reached a given line?" His answer was, "Nobody."

I hope that the truth of our relations with the British and Dutch and the obligations to fight Japan, if any existed, will be fully developed at some time.

The War Department Witnesses

Marshall was the important witness from the War Department. At different times during the investigation the Board called and examined other witnesses from the Department, including Secretary of War Stimson; Former Deputy Chief of Staff Bryden; General Miles, G-2; General Gerow; the Chief of War Plans Division; General Arnold of the Air Forces, and some of lower rank. Nevertheless, Marshall remained the outstanding War Department witness because of the high responsibilities that he owed to the American people. This importance resulted from his official position as Chief of Staff of the American Army.

In the examination of General Marshall and a few others we were handicapped by General Grunert's directive that all questions be written and submitted to them well in advance of their appearance to testify. Every trial lawyer knows the value being able to examine witnesses without notifying them in advance of the information sought. There is no time to think about the answers to be given or the effect of such answers on the witness making them. In the case of General Marshall the advantages of impromptu examination may have been unimportant. He is a very intelligent and skillful witness. This, coupled with the fact that he was the Chief of Staff of the Army and, replying to officers of his command, permitted him to get into the record such facts as he desired the Board to have. Occasionally, when faced with direct questions from which he could not escape, he made direct answers. Generally he was very evasive.

I prepared a memorandum describing the procedure we would follow when Marshall was called, and setting forth the questions that we wanted him to answer. This memorandum was sent to Marshall's office, and a day was agreed upon when the Board, with its assistants, would go to that office to take the testimony.

On the appointed day a small automobile caravan, carrying the above-described personnel, went to the General's office. Since I had been designated to investigate the War Department, it became my duty to examine Marshall. I had outlined very clearly the things that the Board wanted to know from him. The most important information desired was what he knew about the intentions and plans of the Japanese in the fall of 1941 and what part of this information he passed on to Short. We were not deeply concerned about the defense of Pearl Harbor as we regarded their adequacy as unimportant to the main purpose of the investigation. It was my opinion then and is now that neither Marshall nor Short could complain of what had been given them to protect the Navy unless and until they were able to show that they employed such things as had been furnished to them.

After some preliminaries in which the Board and General Marshall passed pleasantries, General Grunert announced that I would conduct the examination. I began by asking questions relating to what Marshall knew about Japanese plans and intentions, referring to the growing tensity in our relations with the Japanese Empire during the fall of 1941. As I now recall, I had asked one or two questions about relations between the War and State Departments when Marshall appeared somewhat vexed by my line of questioning and manifested some signs of irritation at me. In all events, he requested that every one leave the room with the exception of the three members of the Board, A Brig. Gen. Nelson, who was apparently an assistant to Marshall, and McNarney, remained in the room also.

Alone with the Board, Marshall related to us what he described as information, almost too secret for him to talk about. It dealt with the breaking of the Japanese code. Dramatically, Marshall described the transcending value of the information that was being obtained as a result of deciphering Japanese messages.

I am not certain about the effect of Marshall's statement on the other members of the Board. I must admit that I was under his spell. I was very greatly impressed with his descriptions of the importance of maintaining the highest secrecy about our breaking the Japanese code.

I waited with much interest, nevertheless, for him to tell us what the War Department had discovered about Japanese plans and intentions in 1941 by virtue of having access to Japanese diplomatic exchanges. In this field we were greatly disappointed. Marshall used a lot of words, but said little. He discussed a day. This day was a sort of roving day, very indefinite. It moved around in November and finally passed over into December. Something was going to happen on that day. This something would be produced by Japanese activity. What it was, Marshall never said. I remember asking him on two occasions if it was true that the War Department knew that the Japanese were thinking about some day late in November or early December, but did not know the exact significance of that day. Each time Marshall replied that it was true. The picture of Marshall during his secret conference with members of the Board remains entirely clear in my mind. He was a most impressive figure. Words came to him with great readiness. He spoke with a most intense earnestness. I had always regarded Marshall as a very intellectual man. On this day Marshall, the super-salesman, was at his magnificent best.

When he had finished his discussion he sent for the reporters and assistants. When they returned, with an air of finality, he wanted to know if he could be of further help to the Board. In the interim while the Board was reassembling, I recovered from the spell of Marshall's speech and was now back out of the stratosphere and in the Pentagon. I realized that the two main questions that the Board wanted to ask Marshall had not been answered. I remained curious about Marshall's knowledge of Japanese plans and intentions in 1941, and what he had passed on to Short.

No effort will be made to follow the first examination of Marshall, as it developed. Main features of that examination will be discussed.

Relation Between the War Department and the State Department

The relation between the War and State Departments as described by General Marshall was very cordial. Secretary Hull frequently invited the Secretary of War and the Secretary of Navy to the State Department for the purpose of informing those two secretaries of the Japanese-American relations. On numerous occasions both Marshall and Stark were present at these conferences. Marshall believed that the War and Navy Departments were fully informed by the Secretary of State, who withheld nothing of importance from them. No restrictions were placed on the War and Navy Departments about this information. It could be transmitted to field commanders. Likewise, the Secretary of War left Marshall free to deal with Short, prescribing no limitations on what Marshall should send to Short.

Marshall was not very much impressed with the importance of these conferences at the office of the Secretary of State. Secretary Hull, according to Marshall, talked very slowly and consumed a lot of time that was sorely needed by Marshall for his duties as Chief of Staff. The War Department knew much more about the American-Japanese relations than did the Secretary of State. I gathered from Marshall's testimony that such additional information had been obtained by the War Department as a result of its reading of the Japanese exchanges. I asked General Marshall, when he was discussing this, if it was true that the War Department was informing the State Department rather than being informed by the State Department. To this he answered in the affirmative.

I asked General Marshall if he regarded the aggressive attitude of the State Department toward Japan in 1941 as in keeping with the lack of preparedness of our military-naval forces to conduct war. To this General Marshall replied he did not think it proper for him to discuss the conduct of some other department of the government.

Relations with Short

Questions were directed to Marshall to discover whether or not he had sent to Short information other than that contained in the records of the Adjutant General. It developed that for a time, at least, he had maintained some kind of private filing system, separate and distinct from the office of the Adjutant General. From that source he produced letters which had been exchanged between him and Short. In the main, this correspondence touched the question of equipment and men for the defense of Pearl Harbor. The letters depicted a very clear picture of a shortage of both men and equipment. Short was pleading for both. Marshall referred to one of Short's letters as pathetic. Recently I saw a statement in the Press that General Marshall, in testifying before the Congressional Committee investigating the attack at Pearl Harbor, had said it was his belief that the means available to Short at the time of the attack were sufficient to have defeated the attack, or at least to have greatly minimized its effect.

In a letter read to the Board by Marshall, he discussed Short's mission to protect the Navy at Pearl Harbor. In connection with that mission Marshall had told Short that the most serious threat to the Navy at Pearl Harbor was an aerial attack by carrier-borne aircraft. I asked General Marshall if his views had changed about this all-important question in any way since he expressed them in the letter being discussed. To this he replied, "No."

It is strange that during the very same examination General Marshall testified that at the time of the attack he did not expect it. He went further to say that it had always been a mystery to him why the Naval people who, in February 1941, had become seriously exercised about the possibility of a carrier-borne attack had apparently abandoned this fear prior to December 7, 1941. It was while reading these letters which had passed between him and Short that General Marshall read the joint statement to the President, made by him and Stark. It is my belief that General Nelson had handed General Marshall all of these letters and had included the joint statement without Marshall's knowledge. Marshall had begun reading it to the Board, very probably, before he realized what document had been given him.

When he had finished the major portion of the examination I realized that we had made little progress in determining what Marshall knew about the Japanese plans and intentions in the late fall of 1941. So far as the evidence developed disclosed, he had told Short practically nothing. The nature of the examination had been such as to require a complete disclosure of everything that Marshall had sent Short.

Marshall Discusses No. 472

I then turned to an examination of Marshall about the message of November 27 (472) and Short's reply thereto. I do not recall that he described his relation to 472. He was very hazy about having seen Short's sabotage reply. It had passed over his desk. On it had been stamped the words "Chief of Staff." The reply of "action taken" had been sent by MacArthur in the Philippines. On it had been stamped "Chief of Staff", but Marshall's initials in ink also appeared on the MacArthur reply. The initials of the Secretary of War in ink appeared both on the MacArthur and Short replies. Marshall assumed that the two replies had been attached to the same transmittal sheet; that this sheet, with the messages attached, had reached him and had been sent to the Secretary of War. He probably had inadvertently neglected to initial both replies. It was his assumption that he had seen the Short reply. He stated that whether he saw the Short reply or not, his responsibility in connection with it could not be escaped.

In referring to questions about the form and substance of 472, he made the tremendously important statement that we will stand on the record as written. He realized then that he was on the defensive. He did not wish to discuss the probable effect of the limitations and restrictions in 472 on Short's thinking.

Toward the end of the examination, General Marshall lost interest in it. He began to watch the clock rather regularly and stated that he had some meeting which he was forced to attend. It was with important representatives of foreign countries.

When we left his office, I realized that the "brush-off" technique had been applied; that a great part of the time had been consumed by Marshall in reading meaningless correspondence, and all for a purpose.

His description of his actions on the morning of December 7, 1941, will be discussed later.

The Secretary of War

It was the desire of the Board to examine the Honorable Henry L. Stimson, Secretary of War. A memorandum was prepared, setting forth the procedure to be followed in such examination. It included the questions that would be asked the Secretary.

Shortly after the delivery of this memorandum to the office of the Secretary of War, General Grunert reported to the Board that he had been advised by some assistant in that office that the Secretary would not appear as a witness. I have no personal knowledge of the conversation between the President of the Board and this assistant, but the definite impression was given by General Grunert that the Secretary was not interested in the investigation. It was also revealed that he was going away for an extensive holiday in the Adirondack Mountains. It seemed that neither the Pearl Harbor investigation nor the conduct of the War were of sufficient importance to disturb his vacation.

The memorandum that had been sent to the office of the Secretary was placed in the record by the Board. In connection with the memorandum, a statement was dictated to the effect that the Secretary had declined to appear as a witness.

Later, and after the Board returned from the West Coast and Pearl Harbor, Mr. Stimson changed his mind and testified. In fairness to him, it should be said, now, that he made a most excellent witness, giving the Board a great deal of information with the utmost candor and frankness.

General Arnold

The testimony of General Arnold, while informative and interesting, was not very vital in its nature. He described his efforts to get aircraft and equipment to the Pacific. He was outspoken and enthusiastic when he referred to the certainty of the air corps ability to have broken up the attack on the Philippines had sufficient bombers been present on those islands. General Arnold was somewhat different from the average military witness. He spoke out freely and his testimony was not evasive.

He was examined about the failure of the Air Corps to arm aircraft being sent from the West Coast to Hawaii. He stated that the absence of guns on such aircraft enabled these ships to depart with greater quantities of gasoline than would have been possible had arms and ammunition been carried. He regarded the risks incident to limited fuel as more serious than the possibility of attacks by the Japanese. General Short had made much of the fact that the aircraft arriving in Hawaii from the West Coast were unarmed. Orders required that they be armed before their departure for the Philippines and other points farther west in the Pacific.

The Board had become deeply interested in the dissemination of Japanese information to officers in high places. We asked General Arnold if he had been told about the growing tenseness of our relations with Japan. To this he replied that in the fall of 1941 he had thought all of this information was being passed on to him, but comparatively recently he had discovered that much was taking place about which he was not informed.

At this point, General Grunert, apparently understanding that Arnold's testimony was a reflection on Marshall, hastily injected a question. He inquired whether or not Arnold believed that he was given sufficient information about the Japanese relations to permit him to accomplish his mission. Arnold, after thinking briefly, stated that since his mission was to get all of the men and equipment possible into the Pacific, he probably had all of the Japanese information necessary.

General Arnold described some visit that he made to the West Coast and probably beyond during which he was attempting to inculcate into the army personnel a war spirit. He stated he was surprised to find the indifference toward the imminence of war that was so clearly manifested by practically all of the army personnel he saw on this trip. He was very sabotage-minded.

General Sherman Miles

General Miles was G-2 of the War Department prior to and at the time of the attack at Pearl Harbor. His testimony from the stand-point of the War Department was second in importance to that of General Marshall. To me he was a complete washout as a witness. It should be said in the beginning that he was doubtless under instruct-ions from the War Department to avoid giving testimony about Japanese information that was in the office of G-2 in the fall of 1941. Particularly is this true of such data as was contained in the inter-cepted Japanese messages.

His testimony was unimpressive. It was largely theoretical and philosophical.

At the time of General Miles' appearance, the Board believed that the task force that struck Pearl Harbor had departed from the mandated islands. In the Roberts Report we had found a statement that the Navy knew of aircraft carriers in the mandated islands in late November or early December of 1941. Since these islands were nearer to Pearl Harbor than any other positions under the control of the Japanese, we assumed that the task forces had been sent to the mandated islands en route to Pearl Harbor.

In General Miles' examination we questioned him closely about the mandated islands. What did he know about them? His reply in substance was, nothing. Why? Because he had no means of learning just what the Japanese had been doing on those islands. Wasn't it true that under the terms of the mandate our Government and some others had a right to visit these islands and inspect them to determine if the Japanese were using them as military and naval bases? Yes, that was true, but every effort that had been made to have an American vessel stop in those islands had been denied. The State Department required that such request be cleared through that Department. The Japanese would generally accede to these requests, but would always find some reason why the time was not opportune. No such request had been made for some time as the State Department was not in harmony with the wishes of the War Department to inspect the mandated islands.

What about spies? It was impossible to send spies onto the islands
because a white man's life would not have been safe. Did G-2 ever
send anyone onto the islands to look and make a report? No. Why?
Because of the danger involved. How did G-2 know that such
representatives would be killed? Well, everybody knew that.

At this point in Miles' examination, he was becoming considerably confused and appeared very much embarrassed. Grunert came
rushing to his rescue. Grunert, apparently very much irritated by my
examination, wanted to know where I was going.

I questioned G-2 to learn what he knew about Japanese movements on the home islands and in the adjacent seas. He said he was
very well informed. Asked by whom, he replied that the chief source
of his information was the American Embassy in Tokyo. I then read
Ambassador Grew's statement as reported in *Peace and War*. In that
statement Ambassador Grew said:

> We are fully aware that our present most important duty
> perhaps is to detect any premonitory signs of naval or military
> operations likely in areas mentioned above and every
> precaution is being taken to guard against surprise. The
> Embassy's field of naval or military observation is restricted
> almost literally to what could be seen with the naked eye, and
> this is negligible. Therefore, you are advised, from an abund-
> ance of caution, to discount as much as possible the likeli-
> hood of our ability to give substantial warning.

When General Miles' attention was called to this report from
Ambassador Grew, he readily admitted that he knew about it. He
made no intelligent explanation of his testimony that the United
States Embassy was a fertile source of information about military and
naval movements of the Japanese.

Later he said that:

> But to answer your question more succinctly, I do not think
> any Intelligence officer ever thought that he could be sure of
> picking up a convoy or attack force or task force in Japan

before it sailed and know where it was going. That was beyond our terms of efficiency.

It was perfectly obvious to me that in the fall of 1941 the office of G-2 was improperly organized; that it was concerned only with routine matters that could be handled over the desks in Washington. There was an absolute lack of foreign agencies to conduct intelligent investigations of nations with which we were about to enter war. Its utter inadequacy was appalling and depressing.

I saw General Miles on the one occasion when he appeared before the Board. So far as I know, he is a good soldier, but it didn't require any super intelligence to realize that he was hopelessly unfitted for the job of G-2 in the War Department. His approach to the problems of that office was academic and impractical. He attempted to impress on the Board his views of the nature of the work to be done by G-2. It must be that he realized that he had made a very poor showing before the Board. After he had gone away, he wrote a long letter to the President of the Board that he desired to have inserted into the record. As I remember, it contained numerous corrections of or amendments to his testimony. This letter, similar to his evidence, was academic and philosophical. One of the great lessons of Pearl Harbor, one of its tragic warnings, arises out of the failure of our military and naval information agencies. This failure was dismal and complete. We will come back to that later.

General Bryden

General Bryden was one of the older officers on duty with the General Staff at the time of the attack on Pearl Harbor. He was also one of the deputy chiefs of staff who was serving at the time. Marshall had several deputies prior to Pearl Harbor. Presumably each of these deputies was assigned to specific duties. For example, Arnold was deputy chief of staff for the air forces. Some one else was deputy chief of staff for supply, etc.

Bryden was the senior officer among these deputies, hence he functioned as the chief of staff when Marshall was away.

Prior to the time that Bryden appeared as a witness, the Board had learned that Marshall had left Washington on the 26th of November, 1941, for the Carolinas where maneuvers were being conducted. He had returned to Washington late on the 27th or early on the 28th. It came to pass, therefore, that when the message of the 27th (472) was sent to Short, Bryden in his official capacity as senior of the deputies should have participated in the preparation of this message or should have approved it as finally prepared. It was an important message and was sent to Short over Marshall's signature, thereby becoming an act of Marshall.

For the above reasons, I looked forward to Bryden's testimony with considerable interest. Conditions in the War Department immediately before the attack at Pearl Harbor were somewhat muddy at this point in the investigation, though the conclusions to be drawn from what the Board knew at the time were highly unfavorable to the War Department. Bryden's testimony did nothing to clarify the situation. If his evidence was to be taken seriously, his ignorance was dense and amazing. He knew absolutely nothing. He had no recollec-tion of the tragic events of the last days of November and the early days of December 1941. The exchange of information between the War Department and the Hawaiian Department was entirely foreign to any of his experience.

I remember asking him about a stamp in the office of Marshall upon which appeared the words "Chief of Staff." It was material in our investigation of Marshall's relation to Short's sabotage reply. It will be recalled that this reply had been stamped in the office of the Chief of Staff. Bryden testified that there were several of these stamps lying around loose in the inner and outer offices, used by the Chief of Staff, and almost anyone who wanted to use them was at liberty to do so.

When questioned about his approval or non-approval of the message of November 27 (472), he had absolutely no recollection about it. But he did testify that he had been told nothing about the situation in the Pacific and our relations with the Japanese; hence he was not in position to have given intelligent consideration to the message. Imagine the Deputy Chief of Staff knowing nothing about those relations.

It was perfectly evident to me that Bryden, the Senior Deputy Chief of Staff, was purposely evading all questions. He, like G-2, was willing, probably anxious, for us to believe that he was much more ignorant and inefficient than it was possible for anyone to be. I regarded his treatment of the Board as little short of contemptuous.

General Mckee

In our efforts to fix the responsibility for the preparation of the November 27 message, it was discovered that a General McKee, then on duty as an Assistant Division Commander of the 87th Division, at Fort Jackson, S. C., had been in the War Plans Division in the fall of 1941. He was brought to Washington to testify. It had been hoped that the evidence that he could give the Board would clarify the situation, to the extent that General Gerow, who was commanding a corps in France, at the time, could be left on duty with his troops. When General McKee came to Washington, he went to the Pentagon Building and called me from there. Apparently the War Department was then directing senior officers, who were summoned as witnesses, to report first to the War Department, and later to the Board. It might be that such officers, acting on their own motion, went by the War Department to "see what was going on." In all events, McKee called me from the Pentagon and requested that I tell him what we would ask him when he was called as a witness. Since I was in opposition to such a policy, I refused to comply with the request, although I did tell him that I would be willing to talk with him before he testified, if he desired such a conference. In response to this offer, he came over to the Board's office in the Munitions Building, and we discussed the things the Board wanted to know from him.

Immediately, when he was told that the Board was intensely interested in the history of 472, he denied any connection with it or any knowledge of it. He asserted he was ignorant of all the details of our Japanese relations. The colonel, Bundy, now deceased, who has been referred to before, had handled all such details.

In a general way he knew of the plans of the War Department to formulate major policies for the control of the Commanding General of the Hawaiian Department. The Board had been furnished by the War Department with some large volumes in which these policies and related matters had been printed. McKee was able to identify these.

I recall quite vividly one incident that occurred in my conversation with McKee. I was pressing him about 472 and Short's sabotage reply. I was awaiting a remark that would throw light on the preparation of the Marshall message and the consideration that was given to Short's reply by the War Plans Division. It may be that I was a little critical, if not caustic, in my remarks about the lack of information which officers had, who should have been very concerned about this historical period in our national life. I told McKee that these messages were certainly regarded with great importance in 1941 since they had been sent to the Secretary of War Stimson and the Chief of Staff Marshall. To this time in our conversations McKee had appeared somewhat bored and indifferent, withdrawing into the customary cloak of ignorance. When Marshall's connection with the Short reply was mentioned, he manifested the very greatest interest and suddenly rushed to Marshall's defense. With vigor he stated that he did not believe that General Marshall had ever seen Short's reply. Questioned as to his reasons for this, he again became evasive and gave no reasons.

To me this changed attitude on McKee's part and his eagerness to defend Marshall indicated very clearly that he knew a great deal more about the relations between the War Department and the Hawaiian Department at the time of Pearl Harbor than he was willing to tell. It indicated further that the purpose of those in the War Department at that time was to protect Marshall. Notwithstanding his apparent indifference, McKee appreciated fully the situation in which he and others in the War Department at the time of Pearl Harbor had been placed by Short's reply to the Marshall confused message.

We Leave the War Department

We are now ready to turn our attention to the Hawaiian Department. In this chapter, we have outlined the main developments in
our search for the truth about the conduct of the War Department.
If the reader is impressed that the War Department story is not clear,
it will be the same impression, which I, as a member of the Board,
had at this time in the investigation.

One thing was becoming evident. The General Staff, as organized
in late November and early December of 1941, was a curious group
of inactive old men and ambitious young fellows from the schools.
In the main it was a very inefficient unit composed of incompetents
and misfits. General Marshall who had become the Chief of Staff in
the summer of 1939 must be held responsible for this. Ample time
and opportunity had existed for the reorganization of the staff.

4 | Hawaiian Department

The investigation of the War Department, partially completed when evidence of the Hawaiian Department's operations was begun, had to a large extent outlined the pattern for the Hawaiian Investigation. All actions of the War Department relating to the Hawaiian Department had reacted almost immediately at Hawaii. Similarly the things which had been done in the Hawaiian Department had been reflected in the War Department. The two headquarters were inseparably interwoven and entwined in a close combat combination.

The Board knew of many rumors about happenings in the Hawaiian Department. We were anxious to investigate these rumors to the end that the American people might be correctly informed.

Common among these rumors was the report of dissipation and drunkenness on the night preceding the Pearl Harbor attack. This rumor included General Short who was represented at times as having attended a liquor party on the night prior to the attack. Another rumor that had gained very wide circulation described headlines appearing in a Honolulu newspaper a day or two preceding the attack. These headlines told that war with Japan was imminent. By implication, those who repeated this rumor credited the newspaper in which the headlines appeared with having definite information that the Japanese were about to attack Pearl Harbor. In reading the debates on the Pearl Harbor disaster which had occurred in Congress we found a speech by a Congressman from Kentucky in which he had charged that the Hawaiian Department had been informed or could have been informed had it heeded these news-paper warnings. The same Congressman in the same speech, as I recall, referred to the refusal of Short and his G-2, Colonel Fielder, to listen to or even receive courteously a secret service operator who brought to the two officers a report of a telephone conversation between Hawaii and Tokyo on Saturday, December 6. We made several attempts to have this Congressman appear as a witness before the Board. It was our desire to examine him as to the source of his information and learn by such examination if he knew facts in support of the statements made on the floor of the House. The Congressman left Washington for a visit to Kentucky shortly after we talked to him and when he returned to Washington went to a hospital. We pressed on several occasions to get him as a witness, but were never successful.

One rumor, which we left partially investigated, had it that the Australian Government knew that a task force had sailed from Japanese home waters a few days before the attack and after preceding south for a distance had turned east toward the United States. We called some witnesses who had heard the Australian Envoy to Washington tell of this Australian knowledge. One of these witnesses was Senator Ferguson who is now a member of the Congressional Committee investigating the Pearl Harbor disaster. Personally, I was impressed not only with the Senator, but with one other witness who was called. He supported the Senator's recital of facts. Unfortunately, the Australian who made the remarks had left Washington before his identity was known to the Board. It was reported to us that he was somewhere on the West Coast, but was leaving immediately for Australia. This was in October and our time was running out; hence he was not called as a witness.

In our study of the Hawaiian Department we followed the same procedure as adopted in our investigation of the War Department. We searched the records of the Hawaiian Department and introduced in evidence such of those as we regarded material to our mission. In addition to the evidence in these records, we produced much oral testimony by calling numerous witnesses who were on duty in Hawaii just prior to and at the time of the attack.

A semi-humorous incident occurred in connection with our visit to Hawaii. The Board and its assistants left San Francisco by aircraft and reached Hickam Field at Pearl Harbor about 7:30 A.M. For some reason no one in the islands had been notified of our coming. When the pilot of our ship reported to the tower that we were about to land, he was asked where we came from. When we reached the field just after daylight, no one was present to meet us. Some wag in the group observed that this was a repetition of the attack on Pearl Harbor as the Board investigating the catastrophe was as much of a surprise to our forces on the islands as the Japanese task force had been. Shortly, however, automobiles began to appear from many directions and we were cared for.

When we reached the Island, General Grunert, who was investigating the Hawaiian Department, directed that I make an examination of the records for the purpose of selecting those in which the Board might be interested. Very little was discovered that had not been seen in the War Department. We would find the originals of a message that had been sent by the War Department to Hawaii. A copy of that message had been placed in the record in Washington. In the Hawaiian Department we would find copies of messages, the original of which we had already seen in Washington. On the main issues, to wit, what Washington and Hawaii had known and what information had been exchanged, we learned very little at Hawaii. We did find a few letters and training memoranda in Hawaii, prepared in connection with integrating the training efforts of the Army and Navy. These, of course, were interesting reports, since they evidenced a spirit of cooperation between the Army and the Navy.

Some question had arisen about the alerts of the Hawaiian Department that had been published in a standing operating procedure. Conflict had arisen on the question of sending these alerts to the War Department by the Hawaiian Department. It was not debatable that General Short had transmitted them to General Marshall in a letter, early in October 1941. Marshall read these alerts, together with the other parts of the operating procedure, and had made some comments on them, by letter, to General Short. The War Department disclaimed any knowledge of the existence of these alerts. After a rather extensive investigation in the Hawaiian Department it was shown that they were not returned to the War Department by the Hawaiian Department after General Marshall had sent them back to General Short. It came to pass, therefore, that only Marshall in Washington had seen and knew of the existence of these alerts.

Such lack of information in Washington had no material bearing on the main issue as Short had not referred to the alerts when he reported his action taken, in his message of November 27. He had testified that he didn't want any confusion on his message and for that reason had not referred to the alerts by number. He had stated "Command alerted for sabotage" so as to avoid confusion.

To my mind, Marshall's method of handling his correspondence with Short on such material matters as the alerts, without referring them to the proper divisions of the General Staff, was evidence of the charge so often made that he operated the War Department as a one-man affair prior to December 7, 1941.

We shall refer to some miscellaneous documents as we describe testimony that was adduced by Hawaiian Department witnesses.

General Short

It is repeated that Short's relation to the Hawaiian Department was identical with Marshall's relation to the War Department. Short, therefore, was the most important witness examined in the exploration of Hawaiian Department operations.

As a witness, he was the exact opposite of Marshall. Both men have very keen intellects and quick minds. Marshall had employed his to evade direct questions and to give the Board only such information as he wanted it to have. Short testified readily and often too quickly. Sensing the information desired by a questioner, he would interrupt the question before it was completed to give an answer. Some of the record involving his testimony may not be very clear for this reason.

Shortly after the attack at Pearl Harbor, General Short prepared a rather long written report. One of the officers on duty with him testified that he had aided in the preparation of this report. It sets forth in some detail all of the work which General Short did after reaching Oahu in February 1941. He had been very active in building up the defenses of the islands and in seeking additional men and material. He had reorganized the army forces on the island and had initiated very intensive training schedules for his command. In addition to the work which he had done with the army, and there seems to be little in conflict with his claim of stepping up preparation for war, he had worked out rather extensive plans for the safety and comfort of civilians on the island in the event of war with Japan. All of this preliminary planning contemplated that in the event we went to war with Japan, the Hawaiian Islands might expect a Japanese attack. Throughout this statement and Short's testimony before the Board he insisted that he should be judged by the work done during the entire period that he was in command of the islands.

This written statement contained a description of the attack on the morning of December 7. As I now remember, Short was shaving when the first bombs fell. Realizing what was transpiring, he rushed to his headquarters and very shortly, probably in half an hour, ordered an all-out alert. The Japanese attack, according to Short's statement, was very well planned and executed. In its very detail it demonstrated that the Japanese had full knowledge of the exact location of our ships, aircraft and most of our other installations. Japanese planes, especially armed for the destruction of certain types of our equipment, were sent directly to where this equipment was located, for the attack.

It was Short's opinion that his troops went into action after the all-out alert had been ordered very expeditiously, and with little confusion. He was very frank in his testimony that the surprise of the Japanese was complete and resulted from an incorrect decision on his part. He simply pressed the wrong button in ordering a sabotage alert only. He felt that with the information he had, the sabotage alert was the proper decision.

I was surprised at Short's lack of information about our relations with the Japanese in 1941. Even at the late date when he was appearing to testify before the Board, he knew little of what had been known in Washington.

Like everyone else whom we examined, except the Secretary of War, General Short stated that the attack at Pearl Harbor was wholly unexpected and a complete surprise to him.

I recall that I had selected many of the passages from the State Department's book *Peace and War*, which I thought General Short should have known about prior to the attack. I read these to him one by one, asking him if he knew anything about them at the time of the attack. Uniformly he replied, "No." In these quotations, he was asked if he knew about Grew's report to the Secretary of State in January 1941; that in the event of war between Japan and America, the Pearl Harbor attack would be undertaken. To this he replied he knew about it long after the event.

It was evident that Short's sabotage decision on November 27 was based on Marshall's message of that date (472). Short rested secure in his belief that his action in ordering the sabotage alert had the full approval of Marshall and the other officers in the War Department, since it was reported immediately and no exceptions to it were taken by the War Department.

Conflict had arisen between Short as department commander and the commander of the air forces on the Island. This friction grew out of Short's desire to train air corps personnel for defense against attacking ground forces. The issue was not very clear. Apparently the Air Forces thought Short wanted to train air corps troops as infantry. Short contended that he visualized a situation in which all aircraft might be destroyed and air forces personnel would be needed as a reserve for the ground forces. This dispute was referred to Marshall and he had supported the position of the air force commander.

Short was examined about some of the rumors. He testified that he did not recall seeing the headlines in the local newspaper foretelling an almost immediate attack by the Japanese. He knew in a general way that the relations between America and Japan were growing increasingly dangerous, but he did not expect immediate war.

He was asked about the conflicting messages in October that we have already discussed. In one of these messages the Navy prophesied early war, but this estimate was immediately modified by a message from the War Department in which it was stated that no change in Japanese policy might be expected. Short had not been impressed by these messages and didn't remember anything about them when he was testifying. How strange.

He testified that he and Colonel Fielder, his G-2, went to a dinner on Saturday night preceding the attack on Sunday morning, but he was back in his quarters before midnight. This testimony was corroborated by Colonel Fielder and Short's aide. It was my belief, and I assume the belief of other members of the Board, that these officers were telling the truth about the dinner.

We discovered no evidence of unusual dissipation on the part of the Army and Navy personnel on the night before the attack.

Much has been said about a telephone conversation between some Japanese doctor who was a resident of Honolulu and a friend of the doctor who resided in Tokyo. It was this telephone message upon which was based the charges that Short and Fielder refused to receive a civilian secret service operator late on the afternoon of December 6, 1941. The evidence on the treatment accorded this civilian, by Short and Fielder, is in conflict. The civilian testified that when the telephone message between Honolulu and Tokyo was intercepted, he sought an engagement with General Short or Colonel Fielder to inform them about the message. As I remember, he swore that he talked to Colonel Fielder, from whom he received only curt remarks indicating that Fielder was not interested in seeing him. The operator pressed and Fielder agreed to give him a few minutes if he could reach the Hawaiian Department headquarters within thirty minutes. He felt that he received a brush-off from Short and Fielder and that they did not give that serious consideration to this telephone message which its subject matter, and all of the circumstances surrounding it, demanded.

On the contrary, both Short and Fielder testified that they discussed the matter with the operator and were fully advised about the telephone conversation. They thought it might be related to possible Japanese military activity, but they had no means of translating it or discovering its full meaning. They talked about it and went on to the party.

A transcript of the telephone conversation was given to the Board. We read it very carefully. Apparently it was innocent. To me its very innocence was evidence that the language used was symbolic of something else. A code was being employed. There was a discussion of flowers and seasons of the year and what not. I couldn't conceive of two intelligent people spending money to talk 6,000 miles about the things that they discussed. It was my opinion that the telephone conversation was regarded entirely too lightly by Short and Fielder. Nevertheless, this conduct was in keeping with everything else that went on at Pearl Harbor. No one in authority was impressed with the seriousness of the situation that faced the Army Forces there. I have frequently wondered what would have happened had some aviator discovered the Japanese task forces in its assembly position and reported it to the headquarters of the Hawaiian Department. It may well be that he would have been regarded as an alarmist and life would have continued on its pleasant way.

The Sabotage Scare

Short has attempted to justify the sabotage alert in two ways: First, attention has frequently been called to the large number of Japanese people on the islands. They formed a relatively large group of the total population, 33 1/3%. There are three classes of Japanese: First, the old aliens who have been on the islands for many years. There were about 37,500 of these. The second class is made up of the children of Japanese parents who go back to the mainland of Japan for their education. Roughly there are 2500 of these. They are regarded as the potential leaders of the Japanese population on the island. This plan of returning to the homeland for education purposes is considered a part of the program of the Japanese Empire to keep in touch with Japanese people who are living under foreign governments. The third, and by far the larger class, are the Japanese who were born on the islands and educated there. The Japanese at Hawaii were great on organizations of various kinds. The most influential group of such organizations grew up around the church. Here the Shinto religion was practiced and the Shinto priests were regarded as highly influential.

There were reasonable grounds to suspect a Japanese uprising in the islands in the event of war. The presence of so many Japanese on the islands created a real sabotage peril. Much damage could have been done to American munitions and materials of war, as well as to bridges and public buildings of various kinds had the Japanese on the islands been inclined to resort to sabotage.

The facts are that not one case of Japanese sabotage was discovered by the Army Pearl Harbor Board. Many questions were asked numerous witnesses all relating to acts of sabotage, arrests of suspicious characters and trials of Japanese. Notwithstanding this direct pressure for information, we failed to discover one case that had reached the courts in which a Japanese had been accused of disloyalty to the American Government.

The testimony of soldiers and civilians on the islands was not in harmony on this subject. There was a great deal of evidence to the effect that the Japanese inhabitants of the islands were in the main very loyal to our government, but on the other hand intelligent and apparently conservative witnesses testified that the real test never came. This group of witnesses believed that had the Japanese effected a landing on the island that gave promise of success, many, if not most, of the Japanese inhabitants would have joined the invading Japanese forces. According to these witnesses, it was never in the cards for the Japanese on the islands to participate in any acts against us; hence they did not do it.

The second ground upon which General Short has attempted to justify his sabotage order relates to the messages that he received from Washington. Some of them have been mentioned already. He insisted that precautions to provide against sabotage that came to him in messages from Washington influenced him to believe that Washington regarded sabotage as the principal threat to the islands.

General Short described his relations with the Navy Commander Kimmel as cordial and pleasant. They were together frequently and Short was always welcome at Kimmel's headquarters and it was Short's firm belief that Kimmel gave him everything which Kimmel thought Short needed. General Frank pressed General Short at great length in an effort to have Short swear that he had made a mistake by placing too great faith in the Navy's securing Japanese information and passing it on to Short. Short was very emphatic in his testimony about this. He said repeatedly that he was sure that Kimmel played absolutely fair with him, but did admit finally that he might have had too much faith in the Navy's ability to discover the whereabouts of the Japanese fleet and any approaching Japanese attack forces.

Other Witnesses from the Hawaiian Department

Many other witnesses were called who gave testimony about a great many things in the Hawaiian Department at the time of the Pearl Harbor attack and in the months which preceded it. General Grunert having assumed responsibility for developing the Department's operations, did the greater part of the questioning of these witnesses. I believe all of the officers in the higher ranks appeared before the Board. Several in the lower ranks were called and examined.

The dominant question was the state of readiness of army troops in the Hawaiian Department on the morning of December 7, 1941.

Before analyzing the evidence that the Board obtained from the witnesses, it might be well to pause and discuss a question that has been asked me frequently by civilians who are interested in the Pearl Harbor defeat. The question is stated in one form or another, but irrespective of the language used it seeks to know why Short and Kimmel did not maintain an all-out alert during the critical months in late 1941. It will be remembered that the movement of Japanese troops into Indochina in the summer of 1941 created a very serious international situation. Later, and in October, the Konoye Cabinet fell, and Tojo replaced him. The messages discussing probable changes in policy of the Japanese Government at the time of Tojo's promotion, together with such other Army and Navy messages as went to Honolulu, however inapt and incomplete they may have been, should certainly have put Short and Kimmel on notice that all was not well in our relations with the Japanese.

These questioners reason that capable, intelligent officers would have initiated steps to defend against a surprise attack on the fleet at Pearl Harbor by the Japanese. The history of the Japanese nation teaches that it begins war by a surprise attack.

General Grunert who, as before stated, was very anxious to prove all possible derelictions against Short, interrogated some of the witnesses about a possibility of the maintenance of an all-out alert through the autumn of 1941.

I believe that testimony was uniform to the effect that there were insufficient forces on the island to maintain a constant all-out alert. I recall very clearly that an officer of the Air Corps testified that the air forces could not have maintained that type of alert. He stated that after the Japanese attack on the 7th of December an all-out alert was ordered for their forces. Within a few days the men then available were completely exhausted and it was necessary to modify the alert pending the arrival of reinforcements from the mainland.

The witnesses were also of the opinion that a constant all-out alert, even had the necessary men been available, would have interfered most seriously with the training of troops on the island, many of who were badly in need of such training. In addition to the normal training functions on the island, the Department had been designated as a training command for crews of aircraft who were to be sent for service to the Philippine Islands. One of the air corps officers testified that this unit had been depleted repeatedly by dispatching some of his very best men to the Philippine Department. General Short regarded his mission of training as almost of equal importance with his defense of the Navy at Pearl Harbor. The two things, however, went hand in hand.

In this connection it was interesting to discover in the records of the War Department an order of an all-out alert in the islands which was sent to the Commanding General of the Hawaiian Department in July of 1940, and more than six months before Short took command. This order directed an alert to meet an attack of carrier-borne aircraft from the northwest. In the exchange of messages between the War Department and the Hawaiian Department in 1940 we found references to the probable effect on the physical condition and the morale of the troops produced by maintaining an all-out alert for any considerable period of time. It was believed by the authorities in Washington that keeping troops constantly on duty watching for Japanese who never came would lower their morale rapidly. In our first examination of General Marshall we asked him if the effect on the morale of troops resulting from all-out alerts had been considered by the War Department. He stated that it had been given very definite consideration.

No intelligent military man would contend for a moment that a constant all-out alert was indicated in the late months of 1941. I do not think it is debatable that had General Short gone on an all-out alert during that fall and prior to November 27 that such procedure should have been disapproved by the War Department and this type of alert ordered revoked.

The major portion of the examination of Hawaiian Department witnesses concerned itself with the wisdom of Short's decision. I was somewhat surprised at the lack of division in sentiment among all of the officers, irrespective of rank, who were on duty in the Hawaiian Department in 1941. I attempted to account for this on the theory that Short's subordinates regarded such approval of his sabotage alert as a part of the loyalty that they considered was due him. I doubt that this is the correct reason. While there appeared to exist a very great admiration for Short on the part of most of these officers who testified, there was a willingness to become critical of Short at other times.

It may well be that these officers had talked about the attack at Pearl Harbor on many occasions after it occurred. In these discussions they had reached the conclusion that the War Department at Washington had been very parsimonious in informing Short of the growing tenseness of the relation between the American and Japanese Governments. They realized that agencies for gathering any enemy information at Hawaii were very limited, and hostile forces could not have been discovered by the employment of these agencies until they were within striking distance of the islands. Almost complete reliance for Japanese information had to be placed on Washington. They knew that Short had ordered a sabotage alert and advised Washington of that fact. Out of this general line of reasoning had grown a very fixed feeling that Short had been treated badly by Washington prior to the attack and then made the goat after the attack.

The efforts of General Grunert to have these witnesses change their testimony supporting Short's decision was a little humorous at first, but grew to be very monotonous. He would ask the witness if he thought General Short's decision was the correct one. To this the witness would reply in the affirmative. Grunert would then read 472.

In this reading he would emphasize those clauses that contained direct instructions to Short and pass over hurriedly the clauses that contained the limitations and cautions. Having finished reading the message or some part thereof, Grunert would pause and ask the witness whether or not he had changed his views as to the soundness of Short's decision. There were several reactions of the witnesses to this procedure. Some would attempt to analyze the message to make it appear more favorable to Short. Others would express surprise at the contents of the message, saying they had never seen it before. Probably a majority of the witnesses merely repeated their first statement that they concurred in Short's decision and that nothing in the message had changed this view.

There were two or three exceptions to this general approval. I recall General Shaw who, as a colonel, had been chief of staff of the Department when Short arrived to take command. He had served in the Department for a considerable period. Short had taken along with him a Colonel Phillips who, after serving in some of the other staff sections, was made the chief of staff in lieu of Shaw, who was relieved. General Shaw was critical of Short's decision, though he was not present in the islands at the time it was made. He believed that the part of wisdom demanded that Short should have gone on an all-out alert if nothing happened. Based on the experience in the alert of 1940, it was probably true that had Short gone on an all-out alert on November 27, he would have modified it considerably before the expiration of ten days, or December 7. Shaw was a rather conservative witness and I regarded his testimony as sound and of importance.

Prior to his appearance as a witness, I had reached the conclusion that Short had emphasized his training mission in the island to the exclusion of his mission to defend the fleet. I knew how intensely interested Short had been in training the troops at Fort Jackson, South Carolina. It may be that this history had influenced my thinking. I asked Shaw if in his opinion Short had lost sight of his mission of defending the fleet because of his great activity in training troops. Shaw was emphatic in his statement that no such thing happened. He stated that Short was very aggressive not only in the training of his troops, but in preparing for the defense of the island.

The two things were inseparable; the one implementing the other. He stated that Short was in the field a great part of the time, giving immediate supervision to training of the troops and the preparation of his defense.

Shaw was not in agreement with Short's plan of having three types of alerts. He thought there should have been only an all-out alert. In the event it was necessary to place the troops in a condition of readiness to repel an attack, this all-out alert should have been ordered and, as stated above, gradually modified if conditions warranted it. It was Shaw's opinion that members of his staff who were indoctrinated with school methods of training had unduly influenced Short to provide for the different types of alert to lessen interference with training.

One other witness who testified was a medical officer. As I recall, he was the Department Surgeon at the time he gave his testimony. He stated he sensed trouble in the late fall of 1941 and was deeply concerned over the possibility of an attack at Pearl Harbor. He thought at the time that Short's sabotage alert was wholly inadequate.

On other matters the witnesses were in disagreement. It was generally conceded that little preparation had been made for shelters in the event of air raids. Short held infrequent staff conferences. He contacted his senior troop commanders by going into the field and talking with them. Having served with Short, I knew that this was his policy. I did not see the materiality of this policy and, so far as I know, it had nothing to do with the Pearl Harbor disaster.

Short's Staff

If it were possible, Short's staff was weaker than the General Staff in Washington. I remember remarks by the Board to the effect that the one bright spot on his staff was Fielder, his G-2. Phillips, his Chief of Staff, and his operations officer made such poor witnesses that it was impossible for me to know how or why they had reached the positions that they held. The report submitted by the Board singles out and criticizes Phillips, the Chief of Staff. This was entirely justified, but I regarded him as somewhat superior to the operations officer, who by all appearances was the weakest officer I have ever seen in a position of the importance of G-3 of the Hawaiian Department.

The strangest, most surprising, thing in connection with these officers was the assignments that they held at the date of their appearance before the Board. Phillips held an important staff assignment in China, and the operations officer was on the staff of the Third Army, as I recall G-4. Apparently if an officer, through his completion of courses of the General Staff school is designated for high staff duty, it is impossible to remove him from such work.

I recall one incident that indicated to me the absolute lack of intelligence on the part of Short's key staff officers, particularly his chief of staff. It will be recalled that 472, prepared by the cautious general staff in Washington, had instructed the commanding general to "limit dissemination of this highly secret information to minimum essential officers." Such a directive as this is capable of varying constructions. To the secretive mind of the school-trained officer, who had lost sight of realities, and is worshiping at the shrine of academic theories, it meant to let only a very few people know about it. The fact that it foretold a possibility of war, to this type of thinking, mattered little.

In all events, an aide to one of the division commanders (Murray) for some reason found himself in the headquarters of the department. Phillips, the Chief of Staff, removed 472 from the safe and admonished this young staff officer that he was about to give him a top-secret order for transmission to the division commander. He was enjoined to make no notes, but to remember what he was told and transmit it orally to his division commander. This aide was given an impossible task. After hearing 472 read for scores, if not hundreds of times, and having analyzed it very carefully as a member of the Pearl Harbor Board, and notwithstanding my legal training, I would have some difficulty in repeating its contents now.

This aide returned to division headquarters and made an effort to communicate to General Murray what Phillips had told him at Department Headquarters. General Murray was called as a witness. He brought along to the hearing his reproduction of 472 based on what he had been told by his aide. It would have been very difficult to have recognized Murray's transcript of the order as having any relation to the original 472. It is not easy to visualize how 472 could have been made a bigger mess than it was in the original, but Phillips' procedure accomplished just that.

Reconnaissance on the Islands

Three different agencies were active at Honolulu in the collection of information about Japanese activities. They were the office of Naval Intelligence, the G-2 section of the staff of the Hawaiian Department, and representatives of the Federal Bureau of Investigation (FBI). The latter two of these agencies were confined in their activities almost exclusively to the islands. The office of Naval Intelligence had available to it certain information which was gathered by radio interceptions at stations throughout the entire Pacific area. The Naval Intelligence Bureau, therefore, should have known almost immediately of all information thus collected.

It is extremely doubtful that the Japanese were engaged in activities at Pearl Harbor or near thereto which, if discovered, would have foretold the Pearl Harbor attack. The very great secrecy with which the task forces that made the attack operated precludes the idea that the Japanese Navy would have sent information of the proposed attack to any one on the islands, as such procedure might have resulted in a disastrous leak.

There are strong probabilities that in the few days preceding the attack Japanese submarines operated in Hawaiian waters. While the Board was on the islands, in the course of its investigation, Colonel Fielder presented to the Board a representative of FBI. This man brought with him to the Board a map that had been captured from one of the small Japanese submarines, at the time of the attack. It is my recollection that the map was taken from the body of a dead Japanese sailor. The FBI had made a careful study of the map and of all of the entries thereon. So far as we know, the conclusions which had been reached were sound.

The map was of Pearl Harbor and on it was shown the names and location of all of our principal ships in the harbor on or about the 5th of December, 1941. In addition to this important information, the map indicated that the submarine from which it was taken had been in Pearl Harbor for about two hours on the morning of December 5. The story of the journey, as told by the map, is about as follows: The Japanese submarine reached the entrance to Pearl Harbor shortly after 1 A.M. A net across the entrance prevented this submarine from entering the harbor. It waited at the entrance for approximately three hours, and until a scow that at that hour went to sea to dump refuse from the Navy, lifted the net and passed out to the open sea. Thereupon the Japanese submarine entered the harbor and apparently made a complete circuit of the entire harbor for the purpose of gaining information as to the location of the American fleet then in the harbor.

This was a very unusual picture. It was obvious that the commander of the Japanese submarine knew all about the activities of our Navy and like a cat remained at the door to the harbor until it was open and he could go in. The contrast between the operation of the Japanese Naval Intelligence and the American Naval Intelligence was emphasized by this incident. It will be remembered that General Miles, our G-2, testified that picking up a Japanese convoy attack force or task force in Japan before it sailed and knowing where it was going was beyond the terms of the efficiency of our intelligence service. The obtaining of that kind of information about our Navy was not beyond the terms of the efficiency of the Japanese Intelligence.

In this connection, the Board was met with a psychology which, when considered in the light of our relations with Japan in 1941, was difficult for me to understand.

Criticisms of our intelligence work brought this philosophy to light. It was to the effect that after all the United States and Japan were at peace prior to December 7, 1941, and activity on our part to discover probable hostile action by the Japanese would have been a breach of good faith in our international relations. This is a very high sounding doctrine, but in a realistic world it is an extremely dangerous doctrine. While the Japanese Army and Navy were gathering all possible data about us, including the above described visit to Pearl

Harbor, we refrained from watching them for the simple reason that shooting hadn't begun.

If there were Japanese activities offshore prior to Pearl Harbor that would have indicated the approaching attack, they were not discovered until a short time before the attack occurred.

This part of the story is being dictated on Sunday, January 6, 1946. Recent press reports are to the effect that General MacArthur had sent to Washington information recently developed in Japan that indicated that Japanese planes had conducted a reconnaissance flight over Pearl Harbor prior to the attack. Evidence of this flight, if known to the Naval or Army Intelligence, was not disclosed to the Army Pearl Harbor Board.

The evidence was uniform that neither the Army nor Navy on the islands had been furnished with adequate aircraft for offshore and distant reconnaissance. I am not sufficiently familiar with the means available to the Navy for detecting undersea craft to express any opinion as to what could have been discovered about the Japanese activities in the waters near Hawaii had such means been fully employed. But one thing is clear: the Navy was not alert and did not use such means as it had for the purpose of offshore reconnaissance. It is a poor alibi for the naval commanders to say that this lack of energy in conducting reconnaissance resulted from the knowledge that the means available were inadequate.

Radar

A great deal has been said and written about the operations of the radar system prior to the Pearl Harbor attack. The entire subject was dramatized by the accidental discovery of the flight of the Japanese planes at 7.02 O'clock, on the morning of December 7, 1941. In his testimony before the Board, the Secretary of War placed great stress on the fact that General Short had been furnished with certain radar equipment as early as the summer of 1941. By plain implication, if not in express terms, the Secretary of War charged Short with dereliction of duty for his failure to employ this agency to its fullest in the late days of November and early days of December 1941. The

Board spent a great deal of time in the investigation of the progress which had been made in the development of the radar system on the island, the training of personnel for its use, and its employment at the time of the attack. The Wyman-Rohl affair was involved in this part of the investigation.

Radar was new to the American Army. As an example of the confusion in thinking about it, it is quite clearly recalled that for a time, during the investigation by the Board, all the evidence introduced was to the effect that the permanent stations if and when constructed would be much more effective in detecting aircraft flights than the temporary mobile sets. We were told by witnesses that the mobile sets were of much shorter range than the permanent sets. It was deduced from this that the construction of permanent stations on the high lands in the islands was a matter of the very greatest importance. After much evidence to this effect had been introduced and was being considered, we discovered from other witnesses, who apparently were very well informed, that the mobile sets were as effective as the permanent sets and their range was just as great.

Some conflict developed in the evidence tending to show a lack of appreciation by General Short of the possibilities of radar. The witnesses testifying about this charged delays in construction and in instruction of the personnel to operate radar. Viewed in its entirety it is my belief that such alleged dereliction could not be supported by the evidence. Apparently General Short was awake to the possibilities of radar, the necessity for getting such equipment installed and in operation at the earliest time. It was one of the numerous problems with which he was faced on the islands and which he attempted to carry along with all of the other work he was doing. Criticism of his conduct about radar resulted from the enthusiasm of witnesses whose sole interest was the development of radar.

On the morning of December 7, and for some days prior thereto, Short had directed that the radar stations operate from 4 until 7 A.M. He may have regarded these dawn hours as the most critical and dangerous for a carrier-borne air attack. His testimony was that the operation of all radar stations was for training purposes. It was generally agreed that the limited number of sets available to him and the scarcity of parts made a continuous operation impracticable, if not impossible. On this question, as on so many other questions relating to construction and time of the receipt of mobile sets, there was some conflict and confusion in the evidence. It can be said with assurance, however, that on the morning of December 7 there were adequate radar facilities on the island and personnel sufficiently trained had all of this been employed, to have discovered the flight of the Japanese planes when they came within range of the mobile radar sets.

The accidental discovery of the oncoming Japanese planes has appealed with great force to the imagination of the American people. The story has been told so repeatedly that the wisdom of describing it here is very debatable. Nevertheless I have been asked by many people about the incident, some of who had little information as to what happened.

Two soldiers, Elliott and Lockard, were on duty at one of the mobile stations. Lockard seemed to have attained a degree of proficiency in the operation of the radar receiving set at that station. Elliott, an ambitious type of soldier, attempting to educate himself in the operation of the set, requested the help of Lockard. It was for this reason that the station was kept open after 7 o'clock. A truck, which was to have picked these two soldiers up to transport them back to their barracks for breakfast, was late. At 7.02 A.M., Lockard observed on the radar screen what he regarded as an unusually large "blurb." It was so much greater than anything he had seen before that he thought something must be wrong with his machine. He continued to check, however, and concluded that the machine was operating perfectly. It was apparent to him that a considerable number of planes were approaching the island from a given direction and at that time were about 130 miles away. When the position of the planes had been plotted, Lockard called the Information Center and after a short delay talked to a Lt. Tyler, who was the officer on duty at the Center. From the description of what occurred by Lockard and Elliott, considerable excitement existed at the time. Both Lockard and Elliott believed that they had discovered a large flight of planes and that something should be done about it. They attempted to impress the seriousness of the situation on Tyler at the

Information Center. Tyler dismissed the entire matter by instructing Lockard and Elliott to forget it.

I was deeply impressed not only with Tyler's lack of ability, but also with his desire to escape his responsibility for his failure to correctly estimate the information sent him by Elliott and Lockard, by pleading that he had not been sufficiently instructed before going on duty at the Information Center, nor had he received adequate training. He testified that his instructions, when he went on duty, were very general in their nature, but admitted that his only job was to communicate to the interceptor commander information which reached the Center from the mobile receiving sets. It required little, if any, instructions to carry out this function.

The flight of the planes was discovered by Elliott and Lockard at 7.02. The attack began 53 minutes later or at 7.55. Whether or not our planes could have been unscrambled and gotten into the air, in the 53 minutes that intervened between the discovery of the Japanese planes and the attack will always be debatable. Probably General Short's conclusion, that many of the planes could have been saved and participated in the fight is the correct one.

The tragic application of the great secrecy enjoined in 472, the Marshall message to Short, is clearly shown in this occurrence. The truth was that Tyler, knowing nothing of the acuteness of the relations between the Japanese and American Governments, and not being informed that hostilities with the Japanese might begin at any time, was not properly alerted in his thinking and the report from Lockard and Elliott did not impress him. He wasn't expecting war and didn't give the proper consideration to this all-important information that reached him. The correct procedure would have required that not only Tyler, but Lockard and Elliott also should have been informed that war with Japan was imminent and that hostilities could begin at any time. In this atmosphere of expectancy all of the men in the radar system would have been anticipating the arrival of Japanese planes, and action would have been prompt and vigorous.

The failure of the radar system on the morning of December 7, 1941, was inseparably associated with the sorry operations in Washington and on the Islands.

A discussion of the details of the failure is not very enlightening or material.

Means of Defense of Pearl Harbor

The Board did not concern itself primarily with an investigation of the weapons, ammunition, aircraft and other means for the defense of the Navy at Pearl Harbor, but a great deal of evidence found its way into the record bearing on this subject. In the chapter discussing the Navy, we will set forth the evidence given us by Naval officers. Here we will confine ourselves to the testimony of Army officers.

It must be remembered that the assault by the Japanese was conducted by aircraft. No attempt was made to effect a landing. Only those means commonly employed for resisting air attacks were brought into play on the morning of December 7 at Pearl Harbor. The anti-aircraft guns at one time or another engaged in the fight. The fixed pieces were firing early, as ammunition had been issued to them and they were ready on short notice. A longer time was required for the initial employment of the mobile units as it was necessary for them to draw ammunition after the fight began.

No serious complaint existed as to the numbers and types of these anti-aircraft guns. The story of our defensive aircraft is entirely different. Recently General Marshall has testified that he regarded the weapons and ammunition available to Short on the Island as adequate for the defense of the Navy. He said if properly employed, the damage to the Navy would have been greatly lessened, or entirely eliminated.

This testimony of the former Chief of Staff is very much in conflict with the evidence that was given to the board by officers on duty with the air forces on the Island of Oahu. General Martin, who was commanding the air forces at the time of the attack, drew a poor picture of the aircraft available to him at that time. He described these planes as a medley of obsolete aircraft, poorly suited for the purpose for which they were intended. He estimated that 50% of them were generally grounded by lack of spare parts. According to his testimony there were P-26, B-18, P-36, P-40, B-17 and maybe some others. At one time I made a calculation from which I reached the conclusion that in the possession of the Army and Navy there were some 500 aircraft of sundry kinds available to Short and Kimmel at the time of the attack.

When the Board was making its investigation, I had been on duty with the War Department Manpower Board for more than a year. Several months of that time had been spent in a study of the operations of the air corps supply system in the zone of the interior, which means within the continental limits of the United States. I have never ceased to wonder at the numerous types of aircraft that were manufactured for or used during this war. Almost every civilian officer on duty with the air corps to whom I have talked, has criticized severely the rapid change in types of planes which we made during the war. Without exception they say that these changes resulted in confusion, delay and tremendous waste. Here it was at Pearl Harbor prior to the beginning of the War. Unofficially, I was told that it was impossible to repair planes on the island because of the many types involved.

I have little sympathy with the contention of the air forces that a lack of planes on December 7 would have insured the success of the Japanese attack, even if the air forces had been properly alerted and had employed all of these planes in an effort to repel the invasion.

In this connection, I recall quite vividly an experience that the Board had at San Francisco on its way to Pearl Harbor. We had been devoting some time to hearing testimony about the Wyman-Rohl Affair. Much of this testimony was clearly inadmissible, consisting to a large extent of hearsay and unfounded rumors. The proceedings were becoming uninteresting, if not downright monotonous. It was reported to the Board that a young major, who had been on duty in Hawaii at the time of the attack, had reached the building in which the hearings were being heard and was ready to testify. He came into the room where the Board was sitting. His appearance was very unprepossessing and indicated nothing of the thrilling evidence that he was about to give. His uniform was baggy and his hair needed cutting very badly. I had pushed back from the table around which the members of the Board and their assistants were sitting so that this witness was somewhat in front of me after he sat down. It was necessary for him to look backward in order to see me. In his appraisal of the members of the Board he merely turned his eyes in a backward direction and was able to bring me within his view without turning his head. His eyes were very keen.

He testified that on the morning of December 7, he, along with a few other pilots and helpers, were at a temporary landing field some distance from Pearl Harbor. They had gone to that field for target practice. Presumably this installation had been set up after the Japanese reconnaissance had been completed. The witness testified that its appearance was such that the Japanese aviators probably mistook it for something else. In all events these planes were not attacked by the Japanese. When the witness and the others with him heard the firing at Pearl Harbor, they realized what had happened. Hastily taking off from the field they flew to the "sound of the guns" and in a few minutes were engaged in the battle with disastrous consequences to the Japanese aircraft. The number of Japanese planes accounted for by this small detachment is not known, but admittedly splendid work was done.

Before this witness was excused, General Grunert asked him his opinion of the probable outcome of the battle, had all of the American aircraft at Pearl Harbor gotten into the air and participated in the fight. This question of Grunert's was a challenge to this young American major. To the time it was asked he had testified in a kind of indifferent, matter of fact manner. He had recited all of his facts very coldly. Now he was intensely interested. In those eagle eyes was the fire of battle. He looked from one member of the Board to the other, and asserted most vigorously and unequivocally that there wasn't the slightest doubt about the outcome of the battle, had our air forces gotten into it. It would have been like shooting ducks on the pond; we would have gotten them all. The Japanese planes were slow moving old tubs, lazily hanging over our ships in the harbor, and leisurely blowing them to bits.

Later we learned that this officer was one of the outstanding men from the South Pacific. In talking about his appearance with some of their air corps people on the Board, they stated that he was a typical air corps ace. His ability to look in all directions at one time without turning his head was a very valuable asset.

In the long debate which will doubtless result as to the outcome of the battle between the Japanese forces and our planes on the islands had they been in the air, I shall always vote with this young major. I regard the confused testimony of the interested higher commanders as self-serving declarations.

Certain it is that, if our forces on the island had been properly alerted, the Japanese would have met a stubborn defense on the morning of December 7, 1941, in a battle which would have blazed over Pearl Harbor and the waters adjacent thereto, a battle of which the American people could have been proud forever. But we were asleep.

The Civilians, on the Island, Testify

We called a number of prominent civilians who had spent their lives or the greater portion of their lives at Honolulu. They were an intelligent, interesting group of men.

Their views on the dangers of a Japanese uprising were sought. These men had a great familiarity with the Japanese people as they had labored with them and had watched their progress with interest.

Already in this story reference has been made to conclusions reached by the civilians relating to possible acts of sabotage by the Japanese prior to and after the Pearl Harbor attack.

The witnesses being written about, here, were some of the successful civilians on the island. They operated the newspapers, banks, the railroad, the contracting firms and the other important businesses. These men testified very frankly, and it was my impression that they attempted to give the Board accurate and honest opinions in reply to the questions they were asked.

Their Opinion of General Short

There was a great unanimity of opinion about General Short. The civilians regarded him highly. According to their testimony, he had been most active and aggressive in the preparation of the defense of the Island, including many plans for the safety and convenience of the civilian population if war came. He was described as having injected a new spirit into the Army on the Island.

One of Short's enthusiastic admirers, a witness who testified in a forthright manner, described Short's conduct following the attack. He said that the General was about the calmest man on the Island. He talked to groups of people, including civilians. He told them what was expected. This man described Short as a great leader in an emergency. He quoted Short as having said, after the attack, that a message reached the Islands from the War Department in the afternoon following the attack in the morning. Short was represented as having said that had this message come in time everything would have been so different. Doubtless Short was referring then to the Marshall message, telling of the one o'clock Japanese ultimatum that reached Short some hours after the attack.

A Mr. Dillingham was an impressive witness. His father had gone to the Islands as a missionary. Dillingham was born on the Islands. He, along with one or two associates, probably brothers, had accumulated large fortunes and were dominant in the commercial life of the Islands. It was apparent from the beginning that Dillingham was a man of great earnestness and had been deeply affected by the things that he had seen in the Pacific and on the Islands at the time of the attack and in the months following. He too was outspoken in his praise of Short, and his work on the Islands. He said that Short was a most aggressive man and fixed in his opinions. He gave as an example his struggle with Short over the title to certain property that Dillingham owned near Pearl Harbor. According to this testimony, Dillingham had purchased the property many, many years prior to the time Short came to the Islands to command the Department. He had bought it because of his belief in the future of the Islands and the possibility of developments in the areas where this property was situated. Dillingham was connected with a contracting firm and when Short approached him to buy the property in question Dillingham and his associates were about to develop the particular land. He refused to sell Short the property, but this did not deter Short, and, through Washington, Short was finally able to secure title to the land for the Government.

An incorrect picture of Dillingham should not be gotten from this experience. When he and Short were contesting for the possession of the property, War had not come. Dillingham said that after War came, he made available to the Government everything that his companies had, for the prosecution of the War. When his associates complained about some of the things that he was doing for the Government he told them he could not inform them fully as to the reasons which prompted him in making what his associates regarded as sacrifices. He had information that he could not divulge to even his closest associates and told them they must believe him when he said that conditions were frightfully serious.

Another witness, in discussing General Short and the attack, stated that it was his belief that Short had been made a goat by Washington. He gave as his reason that MacArthur had suffered losses in the Philippines, very disastrous in their nature, and nothing had been done about it. He could not believe that Short would have been caught "napping" had he been fully informed by Washington.

In the same connection, these civilian witnesses were asked by General Grunert if they thought that the War and Naval Department had "let them down." There was an absence of bitterness in their replies. They seemed to think that numerous factors influenced the events that led up to and resulted in the losses at Pearl Harbor. They realized there was some difficulty in getting a correct picture of all that happened.

Again, reference is made to Mr. Dillingham. When asked about the reaction of the people on the islands to the conduct of the Army and Navy, Dillingham stated that he had just finished reading Mr. Grew's book, *Ten Years in Japan*. He had been surprised at the contents of that book, the great amount of information that Washington had about Japanese intentions and actions. As a conclusion, he stated that if the admirals of the fleet at Pearl Harbor knew of the things that Grew had written about, he could not understand why they were absent from their ships and in Honolulu when the attack came. This testimony was of great interest to me personally. I had contended always that if Short and Kimmel knew the things which had appeared in Mr. Hull's book, *Peace and War*, and had, with all of this knowledge, been surprised by the Japanese as they were, the punishment which they had received was thoroughly justified. It struck me, therefore, with force when the civilian, Dillingham, reading Grew's book, which in the main followed the outlines of Mr. Hull's book, had reached the very same conclusions.

The Civilians Discuss The Japanese

Reference has already been made to the opinion of the civilians about the danger from sabotage from the Japanese who were on the Islands. The leaders in the commercial life of the Islands indicated a friendly spirit toward the Japanese population. They approached this situation on a high plane, and entertained a charitable view toward the Japanese. It will be recalled that the civilians had great doubt as to what would have happened had a successful Japanese landing occurred.

Dillingham was the owner of the railroad lines on the Island of Oahu. He employed many Japanese people to operate the trains, warehouses and depots for this railroad. After the attack the burdens on the railroad were very great. It was necessary to run his trains continuously. He stated that the Japanese operators of the trains were loyal and worked for long hours without the slightest complaint. They labored under great handicaps, for the Army had issued an order to shoot first and ask questions next. Lights on the trains were not permitted by the military. These Japanese were forced to use flashlights to carry on the railway operations. As soon as one of the lights flashed, it would provoke shots from the troops. Notwithstanding the hardships and handicaps and dangers, the Japanese got the trains through.

Before our visit to the Island, I had talked with an officer who had served in the Pacific with officers who were on duty at Pearl Harbor at the time of the attack. From this latter group of officers my informant had learned that much confusion existed among the troops after the attack, indicating a very low state of discipline and training. I did not expect to get testimony about this from the Army people who appeared before the Board, and it was by the merest accident that these civilians described some of this conduct. The testimony, reluctantly given, indicated troops fired at the slightest provocation and that rifle and machine gun fire could be heard in different parts of the Islands for some days after the Japanese attack. The few questions about this directed to the military people, who appeared before the Board, elicited the expected denial of any such conduct on the part of the soldiers.

The Civilians Describe the Attack

The civilian witnesses told, in a very graphic way, what occurred on the morning of December 7, 1941. One of these men, who apparently occupied a rather prominent place in the community, stated that he had gone to a school which overlooked the harbor, arriving a little early, to make a talk, as I recall, to some of the children who were in attendance at that school. About the time that he reached the school building the bombing began in the harbor. He could see the Japanese aircraft flying slowly and deliberately over the ships in the harbor, releasing their loads of destructive bombs. He described the fire from the anti-aircraft guns near the harbor and was impressed that much of the fire was below and behind the planes at which it was directed.

He told vividly of the reaction of the school children to this attack. They were highly excited and frightened. He attempted to reassure them by telling them that in a short time the American planes would reach the scene and all would be well. Smiling, he said, "Of course, they never came."

As this witness recounted his experiences of that morning and described these frightened children, awaiting the coming of the American aircraft, it occurred to me that the children, looking at the destruction of our helpless ships in the harbor, represented in sentiment the great masses of American people, who were to be astonished and depressed a short time later when the news of the attack reached the mainland.

The Newspaper Editor Testifies

The Board was anxious to know if the newspaper headlines, already described, had been based on information that these newspapers had. The editor of the paper, whose headlines foretold War, was called and testified. He stated that his paper was not in possession of any facts that the public generally did not know. To him, however, the very atmosphere of the situation was so tense with war, and all of the transpiring events were so fraught with warning of war and its immediacy, that it was difficult for him to understand why the military and naval authorities did not appreciate what was about to happen. The conclusions in the headlines were drawn from information of world conditions known to every one.

The Board Returns to Washington

The Board was now ready to return to the States. It had explored all possible sources of information on the Islands. The members of the Board were not discussing the impressions they were receiving from the evidence; hence I am unable to say what opinions either Generals Grunert or Frank had when we finished our work in the Islands. To me, certain things were clear. Prior to the attack, military and naval forces at Honolulu were not war-conscious. They were going along their respective ways, with little thought that War was imminent and an attack on Pearl Harbor possible. This laissez-faire attitude of the Army and Navy forces is difficult to understand. They weren't making the slightest effort to discover the presence of Japanese forces. It is a most serious indictment of our intelligence services that a great task force, with accompanying submarines, could close in on our forces and strike before their presence was known or even suspected. It is a severe condemnation of our commanders, both Army and Navy, whose duty it was to protect this important outpost in the Pacific.

We had now developed definitely that Washington had told Short and Kimmel very little. We didn't know what Washington knew, other than the information that had been conveyed to the War and

Naval Departments about our negotiations with the Japanese by Secretary Hull.

I agreed fully with Mr. Dillingham that if the Army and Navy had been told the things that appeared in Mr. Hull's book, the complete surprise of the attack could not be explained on any logical basis.

In the very nature of things, if War came, an attack on Pearl Harbor might have been expected. Common sense demanded that Short and Kimmel should have been awake.

5 | *The Board Comes Back to Washington*

En route to Washington, we stopped at San Francisco to hear the testimony of a few witnesses whom we had missed on our way to the Islands. We were there for only a short time and learned nothing of importance.

G-2 Is Excited

When we reached Washington I received a telephone call from a Lt. Col. Gibson. He stated he was on duty in the office of G-2 of the War Department, and desired to see me. I told him I was very busy at the time, but would seek an early opportunity to talk to him. The following day he called again and was rather anxious to arrange for the conference. I have attempted to recall the details of my invitation to the office of G-2 to examine some documents that were there. I have a faint recollection of a telephone call from the explosive Clark, but could be in error about this.

It came to pass, however, that I found myself in the office of G-2 reading all of the messages that had been intercepted during the year 1941 as a result of breaking the Japanese diplomatic code. These messages were extremely interesting. To this time I have not seen them quoted in the Press, notwithstanding the fact that the Congressional Committee engaged in the probe of the Pearl Harbor disaster has been working for some months and much of the evidence has been published in the daily press.

These messages were read by me in the office of G-2 in the presence of General Osmun, Col. Clark and Lt. Col. Gibson. The latter officer, incidentally, was a reserve officer who had been in the United States Senate prior to the outbreak of hostilities. I have never known why he was selected to get in touch with me and deliver these messages, as I had dealt both with Osmun and Clark in my futile efforts to discover what G-2 knew about Japanese plans. No attempt will be made to describe the messages in detail. I assume that it was these messages which were being discussed by General Marshall in his vague and evasive testimony about the day that the Japanese were planning against, late in November or early in December. Why Marshall went as far as he did without telling the Board the entire truth remains a mystery. From these messages it could be deduced that the Japanese were extremely anxious to keep America out of the War, but that War was on its way.

Kurusu was sent to America to assist Nomura in this attempt to keep us out of War. One or the other, when it became apparent that their arguments had failed and that America would not stand by and permit further Japanese aggression, admitted his failure to the Emperor and as I now recall there was some suggestion of suicide. The Japanese had insisted upon a meeting between the President and the Japanese Premier. They had hoped to have this meeting at some place in the Pacific. Details for the meeting had been worked out by the Japanese government. It was to be a big show. It was hoped that concessions of some sort would be made which would strengthen the hand of the peace party in Japan. Our government maintained a "stiff neck" attitude toward these proposals, refusing to have anything to do with them unless and until a plan for future relations between the two governments, agreeable to Washington, could be made. When the Japanese representatives were unable to get President Roosevelt to the meeting, they suggested a meeting between high Japanese officials and some one known to be friendly with the President. Mr. Harry Hopkins and Vice-president Wallace were mentioned by the Japanese representatives.

It is a little difficult to follow the logic of Japanese negotiations. It is commonly stated that the Japanese Empire was attempting to lull this Government into a sense of security to facilitate the Japanese attack on us. One cannot escape the impression from the message that the primary objective of such negotiations by the Japanese was to keep us out of the War entirely. How they expected to accomplish this is not clear. Both the President and the Secretary of State were telling them in a very emphatic way that further aggression to the south would create a very serious situation for us, and the President's language on one occasion was strong enough to indicate that if the Dutch were attacked and the British came to the rescue of the Dutch, the Japanese might expect us to start shooting. Nevertheless, it is inescapable that Tokyo was constantly pressing the Japanese representatives in Washington to induce us to stay out of war, and continually reminding these representatives that the time for the accomplishment of this mission was short. It may be that the military party in Japan, then in control of that government, had formulated all plans for the advance to the south and had assigned the diplomatic corps the great task of keeping the American Government from coming to the rescue of the Chinese, British and Dutch. It is most difficult to understand why the Japanese representatives promised the Secretary of State to withdraw Japanese troops from Southern Indo-China into Northern Indo-China and to get 90% of the Japanese troops out of China if the Chinese incident could be amicably adjusted. The approach of the Japanese negotiations to the entire problem is conflicting, confusing and wholly illogical. They were planning to move to the south, while promising to get out of China, when certain things happened.

In one of the captured messages the Japanese referred to America's idealism in its relations with foreign powers. Reference was such as to imply a criticism if not a contempt for our activities in foreign relations.

Pertinent was the message referring to elements of our Navy at Pearl Harbor. It carried with it the inescapable conclusion that the Japanese Army and Navy had not lost interest in Pearl Harbor. Why our War and Navy Departments overlooked it cannot be explained.

I remember the deep impact of these messages on the Board's thinking. They reeked with war. Japanese intentions were clear and unmistakable. Taking advantage of the preoccupation of major powers in World War II, they would grab what they wanted in the Orient. Keep America out if possible. If impossible, it was too bad.

After reading these messages, I told Lt. Col. Gibson that the dirty little scoundrels wouldn't tell us the assembly position for the attack on Pearl Harbor, nor the exact hour for such attack, though they told us everything else.

The Lost Message

Before I had recovered from my amazement at the contents of these messages, and the failure of the War and Navy Departments to transmit their contents, or some part of them, to Short and Kimmel, a most interesting development occurred:

Admiral Hart of the Navy, now in the United States Senate, had been detailed by the Secretary of Navy to make an investigation of the Pearl Harbor affair. The Admiral had apparently done a very excellent job. He had compiled a voluminous document, containing, among other things, a great deal of written and oral testimony. General Grunert made a study of this report and discovered in it the testimony of a Captain Safford, a naval officer who had been on duty in the Office of Naval Intelligence at the time of the Pearl Harbor attack. In the testimony of Captain Safford it was stated that in late November a Japanese message had been intercepted and transmitted, in which the Japanese diplomatic corps throughout the world had been advised that when the home government reached final conclusions as to future activities against Britain, America and Russia, the corps would be notified by the transmission of certain language in weather reports. Of course, this information alerted all of our agencies that might intercept this decision contained in the weather reports. The message came to be known as the "winds" message. Capt. Safford testified that on the night of December 4-5, 1941, the message was received, announcing the Japanese war plans. It contained the statements, "War with Britain, War with America, Peace with Russia."

Further, the Captain had testified that under the plan for keeping the President, Secretary of State, Secretary of War and the Secretary of Navy informed, the Navy was to transmit information to the President and Secretary of Navy, and the War Department was to transmit information to the Secretary of War and Secretary of State. These messages were being intercepted in the main by the Federal Communications Commission and being sent by that Commission to the Office of Naval Intelligence, which in turn passed them on to the War Department.

I regarded this message as of the very greatest importance. If the War and Navy Departments knew on the morning of December 5, 1941, that the Japanese had decided to wage war with America it was our belief that this should have been transmitted immediately to Short and Kimmel, as well as to other important overseas commanders. We sought this message but could not find it. Thereupon, we made an investigation and discovered that Col. Bratton, who was in G-2's office at the time of the attack, had been called back to Washington and was then in the War Department, getting together all of the Japanese messages for the Board. We sent for Bratton and talked to him. We inquired particularly about the "winds" message of December 5. He said that he knew that such a message had reached the Naval Department, and it was my impression that Bratton stated that it had gotten into the office of G-2. I talked with someone in the office of G-2, and he expressed surprise that Bratton had made any such statement. Further investigation developed that I was mistaken on this point, as Bratton had never said that the War Department had received the message. But the story of G-2 about this message was very strange, if not unbelievable. It was to the effect that on the morning of December 5 someone in the Navy Department told the War Department that the "winds" message had been received. It was: "War with Britain and America, and peace with Russia." For some reason it was not sent to the War Department. The War Department attempted to justify its apparent indifferent actions by saying that it requested the message or a conference with the Navy Department to the end that it might see the message. The Navy Department had advised the War Department that the Admiral, who was in possession of the message, was in conference and would be busy for some time. Here the interest of the War Department seemed to disappear. In all events, G-2 was loud in its contention that it never saw this implementing message.

Well, well, just a little matter of Japan's declaring war on us—not sufficient to worry the General Staff.

We had discovered in our informal investigation into this very important field, from which we had been excluded by the War Department, that a Naval officer, Kramer, had been active in translating these messages. We wanted to question Kramer. I went by the Naval office that was inquiring into the Pearl Harbor disaster and talked with one of the officers on duty with that Board. I asked him the whereabouts of Kramer. He stated he was somewhere in the Pacific. He advised further that the Naval Board had already taken Kramer's testimony; that Kramer was in Honolulu when our Board was there and we could have examined him then if we had desired. The Army Board knew nothing of the materiality of Kramer's evidence, as we had not seen the message when we were in Honolulu. We later asked for the appearance of Kramer or that we be shown the testimony which he gave the Naval Board. This request was the only one, as I recall, which was denied by the Navy. We never saw Kramer nor were we given his testimony.

In the conversation with the Naval officer we were warned about Captain Safford. He was described as an officer who had been passed, meaning he would never reach any higher rank than that in which he was then serving. For that reason, his testimony could not be taken too seriously. The emphatic statement was made that the message of December 5, the "winds" message, had never been received.

Captain Safford Testifies

Notwithstanding the statement of the Naval officer that Safford had been passed and for that reason was unimportant as a witness, we called him, questioning him about the December 5th message. He testified that he saw the message when it came in. He was thoroughly familiar with the Japanese language and read it in the original. It said just exactly what he had told Admiral Hart, to wit: "War with Britain, War with America, Peace with Russia." There was no confusion in his mind about it. We then attempted to trace the message and locate it. The Captain stated the message had been in the files of the Navy Department under a given number. Some several months before he appeared to testify before our Board, he had made a diligent search through the records of the Navy Department, and had discovered that this particular message was missing from the files. He swore positively that it was filed in two different places and that these files were in different parts of the same room or in different rooms, I don't remember which. He said the message was missing from both of those places. We asked him if any other messages were missing from the files of that month. He stated, so far as he knew this was the only message missing, as all of the messages prior to this one and following it were in the files. He said further that he had never seen this particular message since it was sent to the Roberts Commission, along with all of the other intercepted Japanese messages. This was our first information that the Japanese messages had been in the possession of the Roberts Commission.

We gave a lot of thought to this lost message. There is no deep mystery about it. It is my personal belief that it was destroyed for a reason. Neither Marshall nor Stark wanted it to be made public. Marshall knew about it. In his testimony he referred to it, saying that the message referred to the breaking of diplomatic relations with Britain and America, and this, of course, did not necessarily mean war. Such evidence was in direct conflict with the positive statements of Safford.

It is my belief that this message was at one time in the possession of the War Department. I cannot conceive of the office of G-2 being so unconcerned about its duties as to sit by and not obtain possession of this message. It doesn't make sense. It would never have done for both the War Department and Navy Department to have lost the same message. This story would have been too thin. It was easier for the War Department merely to say that it never had the message. It could be lost from the files of one department, but not from the files of two departments.

Intercepted Japanese messages had been withheld from the Board by the War Department and I could see but one reason, to wit: Marshall and his close associates on the General Staff did not want the Army Pearl Harbor Board to know that they were in possession of so much important information, none of which had been sent to Short on the Islands.

We called Osmun and Clark to our offices, and all three members of the Board pressed them for their reasons for withholding this information. They assumed full responsibility, saying that no one in the War Department had told them to refuse to deliver these messages to us. I assume that they expected us to believe that wild story. We reminded them that we had pressed from the very beginning for just such information and that in response to our emphatic requests they had submitted to us a lot of other stuff that meant little, but had deliberately withheld everything that was material. They attempted to justify this unusual conduct by saying that they withheld this information for security reasons. Lives of American soldiers would be jeopardized if the Japanese knew that their code was broken. The Board could not be trusted. When it is remembered that many people had been connected with these messages and knew about them, such contentions on the part of G-2 in failing to deliver the information to three general officers of the Army becomes very silly.

It is interesting to note that when we were given these messages it was necessary that a written application for them be presented to the War Department, and no lesser officer than McNarney, the Deputy Chief of Staff, could authorize their release to us. I know this because I sat outside of McNarney's office for a time, with one of these written requests, awaiting its approval by him. The War Department wasn't even intelligent in this plan of deceit.

Marshall Reappears as a Witness

The reappearance of General Marshall before the Board as a witness resulted from testimony given by Admiral Kimmel, who was before the Board prior to its departure for San Francisco, and Honolulu. There was little of materiality or interest in the general testimony of Admiral Kimmel. When he had answered the questions propounded by the members of the Board, General Grunert asked him if he had anything else to say before being excused. This was in keeping with General Grunert's usual custom. Thereupon, Kimmel produced a written statement that he read into the record. It was perfectly obvious that he was laboring under emotional strain as he began the reading. The charges that Kimmel made against the War and Navy Departments were sensational. In substance, they were that the War and Navy Departments knew Japan had fixed a deadline as of November 25, subsequently extending it for a few days, for the signing of an agreement between the Japanese Empire and the American Government, and that if such an agreement was not reached we might expect an attack by Japan. He also charged that the Secretary of State delivered an ultimatum to the Japanese Government on the 26th of November, 1941, notwithstanding a recommendation against such action by the Chief of Staff of the Army, and the Chief of Naval operations. He charged that the War and Navy Departments knew for several days before the attack at Pearl Harbor that Japan expected to go to war with us and probably would direct an attack against the fleet at Pearl Harbor. He said that several hours before the attack came the War and Navy Departments knew the exact time when it would happen.

When Kimmel finished reading, I discovered that both Generals Grunert and Frank were looking at me. Doubtless they were thinking that my investigation of what the War Department knew prior to the attack had been very poorly done. There was certainly some justification for this position, in the light of the testimony that Admiral Kimmel had just given. Since the investigation of the War Department was in my field, I asked Admiral Kimmel if he would reappear at some subsequent time and tell the Board the source of this startling information. To this he replied that to the extent that such testimony would not divulge any confidences, he would be glad to comply with the Board's request. I realized that it was a very unusual situation for a group of army officers to be driven to the Navy Department or its officers to discover things that should have been available from the files of the War Department.

It was my purpose then to recommend the recall of Admiral Kimmel, unless the War Department enlightened us fully on the charges made by the Admiral.

One afternoon during our stay at San Francisco, General Grunert called me into his office, saying he had been reading General Marshall's testimony and considering it in connection with the charges of Admiral Kimmel. Grunert had reached the conclusion that Marshall should be told of the Kimmel testimony, and given an opportunity to refute it or agree with it. A memorandum was then prepared and mailed to General Marshall, calling his attention to the evidence then in the record containing such serious charges against the War Department. Using the Kimmel testimony as a basis for the memorandum, questions were submitted to General Marshall, outlining subjects that the Board desired him to discuss, if he elected to testify again. Upon receipt of the memorandum, General Marshall wired the Board at San Francisco that he would appear before the Board upon its return to Washington.

He came over to the Munitions Building shortly after our return to Washington, but after delivery to us of the intercepted Japanese messages by the office of G-2. At the beginning of his testimony, he stated that upon receipt of our San Francisco memorandum he knew that we had been told about these messages. It was his attitude to place full responsibility for the withholding of these messages on the office of G-2.

On this second appearance, General Marshall, in the main, followed the same policy as when he first came before the Board. He selected certain of the questions in the memorandum and talked about them. I was most anxious that he confine himself to matters which he had not discussed before, and those in which the Board was so intensely interested. It was my personal desire to know why the War Department had sent Short so little of the abundant information which it had, and further why the War Department did nothing to discover the condition of readiness of Short's troops prior to the attack. It will be remembered that Short had reported to the War Department that he had alerted his entire command for sabotage. I thought Marshall should deal with those matters which went to the very heart of the investigation and which would control the Board in its findings of derelictions. He discussed the great necessity for security and the lack of security consciousness on the part of the American people and the Army. He referred to criticisms of our failure to guard military secrets by the British. These were his reasons for not sending Short more information. He feared that the Japanese might break our code and discover that we were intercepting their messages.

After some time, probably two hours of the procedure just described, General Grunert looked at the clock and turned to me and asked if I could finish my examination of Marshall in the fifteen minutes remaining before General Marshall would have to leave to attend another conference. It was the same old story of the very busy Marshall.

I stated emphatically that I had accomplished little and that in my opinion the record was incomplete and would remain incomplete until we had General Marshall's opinions on certain material facts. That I had made every effort to get them to this time, but had been unsuccessful.

In reply to this statement, General Marshall said he would answer any questions that I asked. I then asked him if it would not have been perfectly safe for him to have dispatched the critical information about Japanese intentions to General Short by courier. He stated it would have been safe and feasible, but not wise. I have never known what he meant. He hurried away.

Before his departure, he requested that we prepare such written questions as would elicit the desired information and send them to him for consideration. General Grunert then told me I could prepare the questions that I wanted to ask the Chief of Staff and submit them to him. If they appeared material and pertinent, he would pass them along to the Chief of Staff for consideration. To this I replied that if my questions were to be censored, I desired to dictate them into the record and have them stricken from the record if the majority of the Board thought best. In all events, the second appearance of General Marshall ended with little accomplished.

At this point, I was somewhat disappointed, if not disgusted, with the conduct of General Marshall as the Chief of Staff of the Army. Throughout he had adopted an attitude of evasion and attempted to meet requests for information by speechmaking. I expressed myself to the Board in a very vigorous manner, which probably had some results, as will be noted when we come to tell about his third appearance before the Board.

The Secretary of War Testifies

When the Board came back to Washington, the Secretary of War had returned from his vacation and in some way, which I don't recall, advised the Board that he was willing to testify. He said that he refused to testify when first requested by the Board for the reason that he felt that his relations to the Board disqualified him as a witness. He had appointed the Board and must review its findings. He analogized this relation to the Board as that of a prosecuting attorney or judge to a grand jury. He had before him the memorandum that was originally prepared when it was first made known to him that we would like for him to tell his story to the Board.

He was one of the Board's most satisfactory witnesses, notwithstanding the fact that he brought into play all of his disappearing skill as an advocate in an effort to impress upon the Board that the War Department was in no way responsible for the Pearl Harbor disaster. He talked quite freely about the preparation of 472, the message of November 27. He stated that on the morning of November 25 he was in the office of the Secretary of State to discuss with him and Secretary of Navy, Knox, our foreign relations. He found Secretary Hull in a state of irritation over the long negotiations with the representatives of the Japanese Government and convinced that nothing further could be accomplished. The necessity for additional time to prepare for war against Japan was understood by all. A temporary truce with the Japanese Government was discussed. Secretary Hull was not favorable to this procedure, though he was giving it consideration. At this meeting the Secretary of State told the Secretary of Navy and Secretary of War that he had washed his hands of the entire affair, and it was now up to them.

Apparently November 26 was the day on which nothing definite was done by the War Department, unless a tentative message to be sent to overseas department commanders was prepared by the Chief of Staff of the Army, and his associates. On the morning of November 27, the Secretary of War called Mr. Hull and asked for his final decision on the Japanese situation. Mr. Hull reported to the Secretary of War that he had sent the Japanese a complete statement.

The language used by the Secretary of War cannot be recalled by me at this time, but when we left the office of Mr. Stimson, after he had finished testifying, there was no doubt in my mind that Secretary Hull had reported to Secretary Stimson on the morning of the 27th of November that the statement signed by Hull was regarded as containing the final conditions to which the Japanese must agree if they desired to continue at peace with the United States. Secretary Stimson testified that after he talked with Secretary Hull he called the President to confirm what the Secretary of State had told him. Mr. Roosevelt is represented by the Secretary of War as having said to Secretary Stimson that Hull's statements were true—that the matter had been brought to an end—that Cordell had prepared a fine written statement as the negotiations were ended. No effort is being made to give the exact language of the evidence of the Secretary of War, but in substance he said just what has been stated.

The action taken by the Secretary of War immediately following his talk with the President confirms the fact that the Secretary of War had gained the definite impression that Mr. Hull had submitted a proposal for settlement of our relations with the Japanese which the Japanese would not accept. In a short time Deputy Chief of Staff Bryden and Gerow, Chief of War Plans Division, were in the office of Mr. Stimson, preparing a message designed primarily to be sent to General MacArthur in the Philippines. In discussing this conference, Mr. Stimson said he was very anxious that our Army go on an all-out alert, though the primary concern was with the troops in the Philippines. He insists that he placed the first two sentences in 472. They contained the information that he was especially anxious for the commander to have. When asked if he was shown the message in its completed form, he stated that he was. Did he know the meaning of the limitations and restrictions placed in the message after he had finished with it? He saw these and understood what they meant.

The Secretary of War, in discussing Short's sabotage reply, said he did not interpret the Short reply to mean that only anti-sabotage measures had been taken. Had he placed such interpretation on it he would certainly have objected to the action taken.

In the course of his testimony, he referred to his great interest in radar and the fact that General Short had been supplied with sufficient radar equipment and ample time to train personnel for the detection of the approach of the Japanese task force.

I saw Secretary Stimson four times during World War II, and talked with him on three occasions. I believe he was thinking more clearly and expressing himself better before the Board then, than on either of the other occasions.

We Call Bratton and Sadtler

In my study of the Japanese messages, much of which was done in the office of G-2, I met Colonel R. S. Bratton. He impressed me as a level-headed, conservative type of officer, who was frank and earnest. During the last days of November and the early days of December 1941, he had been on duty in the office of G-2 of the General Staff, in charge of the relations of that office with the Far East. In this work, he had familiarized himself intimately with all negotiations between the Japanese Empire and our nation. It fell to him to evaluate the information in the office of G-2 bearing on probable Japanese intentions and plans. It was his job to transmit to General Marshall's office such data as G-2 thought that Marshall should have. He did the same thing for the Secretary of State.

We called Colonel Bratton as a witness. He discussed the Japanese messages that had been intercepted and their effect on his thinking.

He was testifying before the Board in October 1944, almost three years after the attack at Pearl Harbor. At that late date he was clearly at a loss to understand or explain the lack of action in the War Department, when all of the available information about the Japanese was considered. He testified that in late November he was convinced that War with Japan was a matter of only a few days. Either as a witness or in one of our preliminary talks, the Colonel stated he received a detail away from Washington which he thought would result in his promotion, but he succeeded in having this detail changed because he believed that war with Japan was upon us and proper steps to meet it had not been taken by the War Department. He told the Board in his testimony that he had understood with difficulty our great interest in the last "winds" message of December

5, as his estimate of other Japanese information which the Board had and which had been received prior to December 5, had convinced him that war was inevitable and imminent. His surprise grew out of the fact that the Board was continuing to press for other Japanese information after having seen some of the November messages.

The Colonel testified that he was greatly troubled in November and early December of 1941, because of his inability to arouse the interest of the office of Chief of Staff, (Marshall) and the War Plans Division, (Gerow). He described his efforts to impress these two offices with his conclusions that an attack by the Japanese might be expected at anytime and that our overseas commanders were not conscious of the peril and had not been properly alerted. On more than one occasion, he had conferred with Bedell Smith, who was then secretary of the General Staff, telling Smith about the perilous situation, and insisting that the office of the Chief of Staff do something about it. He offered to talk with General Marshall and acquaint him with all of the Japanese information. He thought that this was very important. Smith had never arranged a conference with Marshall for Bratton, and I received the impression from Bratton's testimony that he was somewhat disgusted at Smith's apparent indifference to the things that Bratton was telling him.

Smith referred Bratton to Gerow of the War Plans Division. Bratton had previously talked with Gerow, but talked with him again. Gerow too was unimpressed and failed to comprehend the full meaning of the things about which Bratton was so intensely interested, and disregarded Bratton's plea for some action on the part of the War Plans Division to convey to the overseas commanders the imminence of war and to alert overseas forces for a possible Japanese attack. The attitude of Smith was that all of the things being discussed with him by Bratton were the functions of the War Plans Division, and Smith was not interested in the transmittal of information to overseas commanders and the alert of overseas troops, if Gerow of the War Plans Division was not interested. How much of this critical information got through to Marshall is something that I never discovered. It is my belief, however, that most of it reached him. It will be recalled that in his first testimony given to the Board, Marshall stated the War Department was fully advised by the State

Department of everything that this latter department was doing, and then somewhat arrogantly said, that the War Department was passing information on to the State Department. His other mysterious testimony in the same connection confirms the conclusion that he was referring to the information contained in the intercepted Japanese messages, when he testified that the War Department was furnishing information to the State Department.

Bratton's testimony about the occurrence on the night of December 6, and on the morning of December 7, was clear-cut, unequivocal and convincing. He said that about 9 o'clock on Saturday night he was in the office of G-2, when he received from the Navy a translation of the Japanese message which constituted a reply of the Japanese Empire to Mr. Hull's proposals of November 26, 1941. This document is the one that was handed to our Government by Nomura and Kurusu at 2.20 p. m. on December 7, 1941. The concluding sentence of this long Japanese message was: "Thus the earnest hope of the Japanese Government to adjust Japanese-American relations and to preserve and promote the peace of the Pacific through cooperation with the American Government has finally been lost."

In summarizing its position in the same document, the Japanese said that Mr. Hull's proposal of November 26 contained certain acceptable items, but, "on the other hand, however, the proposal in question ignores Japan's sacrifices in the four years of the China Affair, menaces the Empire's existence itself and disparages its honour and prestige. Therefore, viewed in its entirety, the Japanese Government regrets that it cannot accept the proposal as a basis of negotiation."

These sentences just quoted are typical of the spirit of the Japanese reply to Mr. Hull's memorandum of November 26, 1941. The document was in the possession of the War and Navy Departments in the early evening of December 6, as has been noted. There could have been no doubt on that evening that the Japanese had regarded Mr. Hull's proposal as an ultimatum and had rejected it. It followed, therefore, that war was the only thing remaining.

Only one sentence of the memorandum was not sent and received on Saturday night. That sentence is: "The Japanese Government regrets to have to notify hereby the American Government that in view of the attitude of the American Government it cannot but consider that it is impossible to reach an agreement through further negotiations." This sentence was little, if any, stronger than the sentences quoted above.

This last sentence was sent to the Japanese agents on the following morning, Sunday, December 7, together with the order for delivery of the entire message at 1 P.M., on the 7th, and the destruction of the code machines. When Bratton saw the Saturday night document, he knew that it was the end and feared an immediate attack. He testified that he placed copies of this Japanese memorandum in two locked pouches that he used for transmitting highly secret data to the office of the Chief of Staff and to the office of the Secretary of State. He remembered going to the office of the Secretary of State to deliver the message and, as I recall, gave the name of the representative of that department to whom he delivered the message. His testimony about his contact with the office of the Chief of Staff that night was not so clear. He didn't remember to whom he delivered the message for the Chief of Staff, but did say that when he left the office of G-2 on Saturday night he carried with him the assurance that he had placed this very critical message in the office of the Chief of Staff.

Bratton came back to the G-2 office early Sunday morning. At around 8 o'clock, or shortly thereafter, the final sentence of the Japanese memorandum was sent him by the Navy, together with the order for the destruction of the Japanese code machines in the possession of Nomura and Kurusu, and the direction that the Japanese ultimatum be delivered at 1 P.M. He then began desperate efforts to locate someone in authority to the end that proper action might be taken. These persons for whom he was searching were his own chief, General Miles; Gerow, Chief of the War Plans Division; but most important of all, Marshall, the Chief of Staff. He called Marshall's home, which was just across the river at Fort Myer. He was informed that Marshall was horseback riding. He insisted that some one reach the Chief of Staff and tell him that it was of the utmost importance that he come to his office in the Pentagon Building. Bratton stated in substance that, having attempted to get something done, he passed many anxious minutes, as a matter of fact a little more than three hours, waiting for the Chief of Staff to finish his horseback ride and get to his office. The last message from Tokyo to Nomura and Kurusu had directed that the code machines be destroyed and their ultimatum be delivered to the American Government at 1 P.M. Bratton believed that this hour, 1 P.M. was a tragic time in American history, and that something would happen at that hour.

He testified that General Marshall came to his office about 11.30. I realized the importance of this testimony, and pressed Colonel Bratton for his reasons for remembering that Marshall did not get to his office until 11.30. Bratton said he could not forget as he had walked up and down in Marshall's outer office, with his watch in his hand, as the precious minutes ran away. When Marshall finally arrived, he handed him the information that had reached him on Sunday morning. As the Japanese were very probably checking their orders, and making final inspections of their equipment, preparatory for the flight to Pearl Harbor, the one man in our Army who could and would act, was horseback riding.

We shall return to these incidents when we discuss Marshall's testimony in his third and final appearance before the Board. At that time we shall contrast Bratton's testimony with that of Marshall.

Much has been said about the failure to promote Colonel Bratton and Colonel Sadtler. We know nothing of the reasons for continuing them in their grades of colonel, but we do recall that in one of our informal conversations some officer stated that the pattern was perfectly clear. If an officer wanted to be condemned forever it was only necessary for him to have guessed Pearl Harbor correctly.

Colonel Sadtler

Colonel Sadtler was a signal officer, and in the critical days before Pearl Harbor was Chief of the Message Center. On several occasions prior to his appearance before the Board we had been told that he knew a lot which would be helpful to the Board. Bratton referred to Sadtler in our contacts with him, and we decided to call Sadtler as a witness. Sadtler added little to the evidence that had been given by Colonel Bratton. The materiality of his testimony resulted from the very complete way in which he confirmed the statements of Colonel Bratton. He had read the intercepted Japanese messages and had made the proper distribution of them to the War Department. To him, these messages were conclusive of the Japanese determination to go to War. Sadtler, as Chief of the Message Center in the War Department, had access to all of the interchange of information between that Department and the overseas commanders. In this way, he was able to contrast the spirit of war in the Japanese messages with a lack of war consciousness in the written memoranda passing between Washington and the officers in the field. Like Bratton, he was intensely stirred by the failure of the War Department and the overseas department to appreciate the very serious situation that faced this country. And like Bratton also, he attempted to do something about it.

He went to Gerow and insisted that steps be taken to arouse the interest of the overseas commanders and to ready our forces in these outposts for war. Gerow was just as indifferent to Sadtler as he had been to Bratton. Following in the footsteps of Bratton, Sadtler went to Bedell Smith, telling him that something should be done because war was coming. Again Smith asked Sadtler if he had discussed the matter with Gerow. When told that he had, Smith said that as head of the War Plans Division, it was Gerow's job to supervise the operations of our overseas forces and the office of the Chief of Staff would not interfere with this function of the War Plans Division. Sadtler went back to Gerow in an effort to get action, and again his efforts were futile. Thus, it was that these two officers, thinking clearly, had reached sound and inescapable conclusions as a result of their analysis of the information in the possession of the War Department, but could get nothing done.

Their conversations and testimony were very impressive of the disgust that they felt at the indifference of the key staff officers in the War Department toward our international situation in late November and early December of 1941.

General Gerow

General Gerow was a graduate of Virginia Military Institute, the same college at which General Marshall had been educated. He had left the War Plans Division when the Board was making its investigation, and was then commanding a corps in combat on the Western Front. The wisdom of requiring him to leave his command was debatable. It was doubted that General Eisenhower would approve a leave for him to appear in Washington. Since he was regarded as a part of the War Department, it fell to me to recommend to the other members of the Board whether or not we would ask that Gerow be made available to us. In making the decision for the recommendation, I was influenced largely by two factors: First, we had learned little about the preparation of the message of November 27, 1941, (472), and since Gerow as Chief of the War Plans Division was charged with the responsibility for the preparation of the message, he was regarded as a most important witness on this vital document.

In the second place, his testimony before the Roberts Commission had been studied, and I regarded it as very unsatisfactory. Mr. Justice Roberts questioned General Gerow about Short's reply to this message. At first Gerow stated that he did not regard the sabotage report as a reply to 472, but on the contrary thought that Short was referring to the sabotage messages, which reached the Hawaiian Department from different sources. Justice Roberts then called his attention to the fact that in Short's reply he referred to the November 27 message by its number 472. Gerow apparently being without any adequate explanation of the failure of the War Plans Division to take appropriate action on Short's reply, in event disagreement with it existed, admitted very frankly to the Roberts Commission that apparently the War Plans Division had simply overlooked the importance of the reply. In other words, Gerow and his assistants had simply "missed the boat."

Another interesting phase of Gerow's testimony before the Roberts Commission referred to that part of the message that directed reconnaissance. He was pressed very vigorously by General McNarney, a member of the Roberts Commission, about this sentence in the order. It was clearly McNarney's purpose to show that Short had willfully disobeyed that part of the order. This examination of Gerow by McNarney indicated to me that McNarney was very anxious to place the blame for Pearl Harbor on Short, insofar as any army dereliction existed. Establishment of the willful disobedience of War Department orders would go a long way in accomplishing this purpose. After some hedging and squirming before the Roberts Commission, Gerow halfheartedly admitted that failure of Short to take reconnaissance measures was a violation of an order.

Gerow made a most unfavorable impression on me when he appeared before the Board. It will be recalled that high-ranking officers who appeared before the Board spent some time in the Pentagon Building after reaching Washington and before testifying. Gerow followed this procedure and called me from the Pentagon, requesting a copy of the questions that would be propounded to him when he testified. I refused to furnish these questions. Later, I learned from friends in the Pentagon Building that Gerow was about the halls and offices of this building for some two or three days before he testified. During this period he was "sounding off" rather vociferously and somewhat angrily about being recalled from the theatre of operations when he regarded himself as so badly needed by his corps. Apparently the Pearl Harbor investigation was of little importance.

When he reached the Board in the afternoon he insisted that we finish with him as quickly as possible, saying he had been in France and had had no opportunity to visit his people since he went overseas. He was in a very big hurry.

It may be that his history as an officer in the American Army justified his being placed in the important positions that he held in 1941, as Chief of War Plans Division. His appearance before the Army Pearl Harbor Board certainly did not show his fitness for any such assignment.

We now learned the entire history of 472. Prior to General Marshall's departure for the Carolina maneuvers, some work had been done on a tentative message for overseas commanders. Presumably this work was the result of the statement of Secretary Hull on the

25th of November that negotiations with the Japanese representatives were about at an end and the entire Japanese affair would be referred to the War and Navy Departments, to wit, the Army and Navy. Whatever this preliminary history may have been, Gerow testified that on the morning of the 27th of November he was called into the office of Secretary Stimson. As I remember, he took two or three people with him and found the non-committal Bryden already with the Secretary of War. He read a rough sketch of the message that had been prepared. The opening sentence of the message as thus prepared stated that negotiations with the Japanese had ended. When this sentence was read to the Secretary of War, Mr. Stimson called the Secretary of State to determine whether or not the statement that negotiations with the Japanese had ended was entirely accurate. The Secretary of State told Mr. Stimson that such negotiations had ended to all intents and purposes, though there was the barest possibility that the Japanese might come back and offer to continue negotiations.

The opening sentence of this critical message conformed to this statement of Secretary Hull. Mr. Stimson had previously testified that he insisted on the first two sentences of 472. He did this because he was extremely anxious that overseas departments be completely alerted, using the term "to be on the qui vive." Gerow then told of the subsequent conferences which he held with the Navy, with General Miles, G-2, and finally of a discussion of the message at a conference late in the afternoon when interested officers of most of the sections of the War Department were present. As I remember now, the Air Forces were represented at this meeting or had been consulted during the day.

It was perfectly obvious that 472 was a hash which had been brewed by a lot of cooks about the War Department. Everybody apparently had his say. This may account for the weak, confused and conflicting message that resulted.

We examined General Gerow about the details of the message. No effort will be made here to discuss his testimony in detail. To me it was very unsatisfactory and demonstrated quite clearly Gerow's unfitness for the place that he held as Chief of War Plans Division.

We pressed him about Short's sabotage reply. He abandoned his statement before the Roberts Commission that the War Plans Division had simply failed properly to appreciate the force and effect of that reply, and now had a queer explanation of the conduct of the War Plans Division. He stated that broad general policies for governing the relations between the War Department and the Hawaiian Department had been established by the War Department. Under these policies the War Department would not interfere with Short as Commanding General of the Hawaiian Department in his training and command of that department, unless his actions were in conflict with these broad policies. In effect he contended that it was Short's job to command the Hawaiian Department and it would be an invasion of his prerogative as such commander to disagree with the decision which Short had made to limit his preparations for war to issuing only a sabotage alert. Of course, in a matter of such vital importance this contention of Gerow was childish, if not downright foolish. He attempted to analogize Short's relations with the War Department to his relation to his Army Commander in France. He testified that his Army Commander ordered him to attack an objective within a certain zone of action. All of the details were for him. The more Gerow talked the more embarrassed he became. I abandoned my questioning of him when I saw that his responses were so ridiculous as to be of no help to the Board.

It was obvious that he had given considerable thought to his relations to the message of November 27, and Short's reply. We asked him why he inserted in the November 27 message that Short was to report action taken unless he expected to follow up such action and determine if it was in keeping with the War Plans Division conception of what Short should do. He gave the rather senseless answer that the War Plans Division had experienced difficulty in getting acknowledgment of messages sent overseas and if he required Short to report action taken this would signify that Short had received the message. He could not explain why he didn't merely say "acknowledge receipt."

It was important to know that when General Marshall returned from the Carolina maneuvers and on the morning of November 28, Gerow submitted a written report to Marshall of what had happened the day before on the situation in the Orient. He attached to this report a copy of one or more of the messages which had gone to the overseas departments. Whether 472 or the one to MacArthur is not material, as they both were substantially the same. Since Short had sent his sabotage alert reply on the afternoon of November 27 and this reply had gone over to the office of Chief of Staff, it came to pass that General Marshall had on his desk on November 28, 1941, copies of the messages to the overseas departments, and Short's reply of action taken. He was in position to, and had the responsibility of, considering the two things together.

General Marshall's Final Appearance

In compliance with General Grunert's instructions, I prepared questions to be answered by General Marshall. They were in writing and sent to the office of the Chief of Staff. This procedure, from the beginning, was very distasteful to me. Since the Board had gotten so much material information, and Marshall had become so involved in the Pearl Harbor disaster, I could see no good reason for continuing to baby him. Nevertheless I wanted to get his definite statements in the record on the few material things which we now knew had caused or contributed to the Pearl Harbor disaster. After a long investigation and a consideration of a lot of immaterial data, the Board had about reached the heart of the entire matter.

The Board and its assistants went to the office of the Chief of Staff. His attitude and conduct were entirely different from that on the two previous occasions when he had appeared as a witness. No longer was he the talkative salesman. Now he was the somewhat irritated executive, very brusque and direct in his answers, employing just as few words as possible. Apparently my criticisms of General Marshall about his treatment of the Board had reached him.

One of the questions related to the joint note sent to the President by Marshall and Stark on the 27th of November. It will be recalled that in that memorandum Marshall and Stark had stated that the American, British and Dutch, in conference, had agreed that no counter-military measures be taken against the Japanese until the

Japanese armed forces crossed a line described as west of 100° east, and south of 10° north. I asked General Marshall who was authorized to make an agreement with the British and Dutch for our Government to take counter-military measures when the Japanese armed forces crossed this line. His answer was, "No one." I regretted then and regret now that his answer was so short, and left so much to be desired. However, he was reading the questions that I had prepared and was giving the replies at the end of each question. We weren't permitted to examine him orally, as regrettable as that was.

Turning to 472, the message of November 27, he was asked if in his opinion that message contained all of the enemy information and all of the instructions to Short necessary for Short's accomplishment of his mission. The answer was, "Yes." It had been my hope that he would discuss this message. His name appeared on the message and the Board should have had his views as to its clarity and completeness. Evidently he had not changed his views since his first appearance before the Board. He testified then, as has already been stated, that they, referring to Marshall and his associates, would stand on the record as written.

He was then asked if in his opinion 472 was misunderstood and improperly interpreted by General Short, thereby failing in its accomplishment of the purpose intended. This elicited another categorical, "Yes." The next question, in his opinion, was Short's reply to 472 misunderstood or improperly interpreted in the War Department, thereby failing in its accomplishment of the purpose intended. To this Marshall answered rather evasively. The substance of the reply was that the Short message might not have been properly handled in the War Department. He had seen those two questions and, of course, knew the implications of his giving the identical answer to both of them. He avoided doing that.

Next, did he know the condition of readiness of Short's forces between November 27 and December 7, 1941? He did not.

Did he make any investigation to determine the condition of readiness of Short's troops during that period? He did not.

We were anxious to get additional information on the meaning of placing the stamp of the Chief of Staff on Short's reply. Previously he had explained that presumptively he had seen Short's reply and had told us why he thought his pen or pencil notation was not entered. In this connection, we asked if the appearance of the stamped words "Chief of Staff" on Short's message indicated to other staff members that the Chief of Staff had seen the message and noted its contents. To this he replied that it did.

On different occasions we had discussed the events of Sunday morning, December 7, with General Marshall. Originally he had testified that in keeping with his usual custom he came down to the War Department about 10.30 or 11 o'clock. Nothing was said about his having received a message that it was very urgent for him to hasten to his office. When he reached his office on that morning, he found on his desk that part of the memorandum of the Japanese rejecting Mr. Hull's proposals that had been received on the previous Saturday evening. For some reason, the final sentence of that memorandum and the order for delivery of the ultimatum, and breaking of the code machines, which had been received early Sunday morning, had been placed on his desk under the longer and less material memorandum.

It was obvious that Marshall was stating his own defense in his oral testimony by failing to tell us that the message requesting that he go to his office immediately had been received. In this final testimony he said that he did not get Bratton's message until he was coming out of the shower bath. Describing the ride that he took as lasting about an hour, it was his opinion that he received Bratton's message about 9.30. He didn't attempt to account for the two hours that elapsed from the time he finished his bath until he was in his office. Only a few minutes was required to drive from his home to his office.

In another very material way, Marshall's testimony was in conflict with that of Bratton. Marshall testified that the Sunday morning message was on his desk under the Saturday night memorandum. Bratton was positive in his testimony that he had the Sunday morning message in his hand when Marshall came in and handed it to Marshall. Marshall testified that he called Stark on the telephone and learned that Stark also had before him the Saturday night memorandum, and the Sunday morning message. Stark didn't propose to do anything about them. No wonder the Navy Board found that Stark should never hold a position in the Navy again which required the exercise of superior judgment. In all events, Marshall disagreed with Stark, and hurried messages away to the overseas departments. He telephoned the Philippines because he expected the attack to be in that area. He wrote the message to Short and directed the signal officer to transmit it as quickly as possible. Some difficulty had been experienced in getting Honolulu on the radio and commercial telegraph and cables were employed to notify Short of what had reached the War Department the night before, and early Sunday morning. When this message reached Honolulu it was delivered to a boy to be carried to Short's headquarters some four or five miles away. The boy was pedaling a bicycle along the Hawaiian road with this message when the bombs began to fall.

One of our last questions to General Marshall on his third appearance was, "Who relieved General Short?" To this he replied, "I did", and then added, "with the approval of the Secretary of War." He was asked for a copy of the order. Petulantly, he threw it across the desk to me. It was a very brief order relieving Short, signed "Marshall." To me this was the most disappointing act that the investigation had developed. I expected him to testify in reply to the question, "Who relieved Short", that either he relieved him or that he relieved him under the direction of the President. Every one in the Army, who was familiar with conditions in the War Department and the relation between Mr. Stimson and the Chief of Staff Marshall, knew that Marshall's statement that Short was relieved with the consent and approval of the Secretary of War was, insofar as it related to the consent of the Secretary of War, a feeble defense based on an effort to pass part of the responsibility for Short's relief to the Secretary of War. Marshall knew that his derelictions were equal to or greater than those of Short, and that military men, so long as they studied the catastrophe of Pearl Harbor, would censure Marshall's conduct in protecting his own official life by destroying that of his subordinate Short. If the Secretary of War could be made a party to the decision, Marshall's guilt in connection with Short's relief would be somewhat lessened. The truth of the matter is that the Secretary of War participated in the preparation of 472, and had seen Short's reply to the message. He too was guilty of dereliction and needed a defense badly. But more important is the fact that to all intents and purposes Marshall was not only the Chief of Staff, but the Secretary of War also. Mr. Stimson's childlike faith in and devotion to General Marshall remains a very great mystery to me, explainable only by the fact that he was very old and had been recalled to the important post of Secretary of War from a life of partial, if not complete retirement.

Only a few days before Marshall testified about the approval of Short's removal by the Secretary of War, Mr. Stimson had told the Board that never at any time during World War II had he made any suggestions to General Marshall about the assignment of commanders or their relief. He had remained entirely aloof in these matters and left them exclusively to General Marshall.

The atmosphere in the Chief of Staff's office on this my last visit to it was very tense. Everyone was tense, but the Chief of Staff's reactions to the Board's procedure was very clear. It was one of deep, but restrained hostility.

I must admit that I was very much depressed as General Grunert and I drove back from the Pentagon to the Munitions Building. It seemed to me that our investigation had disclosed that leadership in the American Army was on a very low basis. En route to the Munitions Building, we passed the Memorial to President Lincoln. This Memorial is one of the impressive and inspiring places in our country. The spirit of Lincoln is very real. You can almost feel his presence when you are there. It ranks along with Jamestown in Virginia, and Washington's Tomb at Mount Vernon.

I have never visited this Memorial without living again in memory those tragic years when the North and South were fighting. Always, I remember other great figures of those turbulent times. On this day, as we passed the Memorial, I recalled the picture of General Lee at Gettysburg. Walking on that battlefield, doubtless realizing the struggle between the Federals and Confederates, which had just been fought, was an end to the Southern Confederacy, he must have known that history would search for the causes of the failures, Lee, with admirable courage reflecting a great character, said, "It was all my fault." History does not agree with General Lee, and has written an entirely different verdict. Contrast that with the conduct of

Marshall. His derelictions in the Pearl Harbor disaster were greater than those of Short, but Marshall's verdict was "It's all your fault, get out."

Two defendants, Marshall and Short, were standing at the Bar of Public Opinion, for trial. One of the defendants, Marshall, having that power, judged Short guilty and executed him to draw attention away from himself.

Lee had the first great requisite of leadership—character. He never understood why men regarded him so highly and followed him so unquestioningly. It was not necessary to establish a tremendous propaganda machine to impress those about Lee with his greatness.

I can't conceive of any of the leaders of our Civil War—Grant, Jackson, and others—atoning for their own sins by sacrificing others.

But our Army had changed; our concepts of leadership in the Army are different.

6 | *The Navy*

A rather long procession of admirals, rear admirals and commanders passed before the Army Pearl Harbor Board. Generally, they were interesting men, most of them giving the impression of having served in their high ranks for some time.

Those who had been on duty at Pearl Harbor and in the Naval district in the Islands were unanimous in their testimony as to the friendly relations between the Army and Navy at the time of the Japanese attack. Some of them were very vigorous in their denunciations of the lack of harmony between the Army and Navy in the years preceding the attack. Kimmel was in this group. They apparently referred to the old days when the Navy went to Pearl Harbor to establish that outpost. Kimmel and the officers of his command and staff confirmed the testimony of the army officers that he and Short were on the very best of terms prior to and at the time of the Pearl Harbor attack.

Their evidence was not convincing of any well-coordinated practical plan for the operation of the Army and Navy forces in the islands. They described all of the numerous papers that existed providing for the joint operations of the two forces. These have been referred to before.

It is my belief that entirely too much emphasis has been placed on the absence of Army-Navy cooperation. The very nature of things indicated what each should do. For example, distant reconnaissance for the discovery of Japanese naval task forces was the proper function of the Navy. The contentions that have appeared from time to time from Naval sources that the surprise element in the attack at Pearl Harbor resulted wholly from Army derelictions is unworthy of the Navy. It is not debatable that Pearl Harbor was established not only as an outpost for the protection of the western coast of the

United States, but also as a rendezvous for the Navy to which elements of the Pacific fleet could go for rest and recreation after maneuvers and operations at sea. As said before in this story, it was the function of the Army personnel in the islands to protect the fleet when in the harbor. This protection was necessarily limited in its scope and envisioned defense against the type of attack that Army ground and air forces were equipped to defeat. It is well known that after aircraft is in flight it is almost impossible to prevent it from accomplishing considerable damage. It is only when the plane is driven from the sky that targets are safe and free from any damage at all.

It follows, therefore, that when the Navy permitted the Japanese task force to bring its aircraft within range of Pearl Harbor some damage to the fleet was inevitable.

Considered in its proper aspects, the attack at Pearl Harbor was a naval engagement. The task forces that conducted the attack were from the Japanese Navy. The purpose of the attack was to destroy our Pacific Fleet. Everything else was incidental. Our fleet at Pearl Harbor was completely surprised by a part of the Japanese fleet. It was a naval engagement in which a part of the Japanese Navy defeated a part of the American Navy because that part of the Navy that was defeated was asleep. It is a very poor alibi for our naval commanders to take the position that their reverses at Pearl Harbor resulted entirely from failure of the Army forces on the Island of Oahu to protect the ships at Pearl Harbor.

The testimony of the Navy was to the effect that for many weeks during the year 1941 the whereabouts of a substantial part of the Japanese Navy was wholly unknown to our Naval intelligence. Recent testimony before the Congressional committee charges that Admiral Kimmel expressed a great surprise when his Naval Intelligence told him of this condition. We have already described Japanese submarines lurking around the Hawaiian Islands. Why our Navy did not have some observation in Japanese waters has never been explained. The excuse that we were at peace with Japan is unsatisfactory.

There was another feature of the Naval testimony that did not reflect credit on our naval forces. Two naval officers in Hawaii were rather emphatic in their statements that the elements of our Navy at Pearl Harbor would have been defeated had they gone to sea and engaged the Japanese task force. They accounted for this in more than one way. They stated that the great number of carrier-borne aircraft with the task force would have destroyed the battle ships and other surface craft stationed at Pearl Harbor before these ships could have come within range of the task force. The philosophy of this testimony is that if we went to sea we were going to be beaten, so we might as well have remained in the harbor, and saved all the trouble. This is of a piece with the Army testimony that complained of the inadequacy of planes and weapons to repel the Japanese attack.

The Army and Navy will never be able to persuade the American people that the disastrous defeat at Pearl Harbor was inevitable because of the lack of means for the defense of the islands. It may well be that considerable damage would have been done to the fleet and our installations on the islands, in all events. It is nevertheless very true that if our forces on the island, both Army and Navy, had been alerted and had entered the engagement in full force, all of the humiliating destruction would not have occurred.

The testimony of Captain Layton was referred to in the report made by the Army Pearl Harbor Board. This naval officer stated that the psychology of the soldier and sailor in the islands contributed largely to our defeat. When questioned as to the meaning of this contention, the officer said some of our aircraft returning to the islands met Japanese attacking forces and were shot down, without any effort to defend themselves. I could not agree with this theory. If American aviators failed to shoot back, it was because they were not alerted by higher authority and were taken completely by surprise. It is impossible for me to imagine a mental condition of young Americans that would prevent them from shooting at Japanese who had opened fire on them.

Naval Organization

The organization of the Navy in the Islands was complicated and difficult for an Army officer to understand. There were a lot of papers and a lot of admirals for the size of naval forces involved. Whether this complicated set-up and all of the papers had any material effect on the operations prior to and at the time of the attack is extremely doubtful.

The joint plans for the operations of the Army and Navy published, as I recall, in 1935 required that local commanders in the Hawaiian Islands work out plans for the operations of those elements of the Army and Navy stationed in the islands. They were typical Army and Navy papers, voluminous but probably never read nor seriously considered after being prepared. It was the old, old game of the two services working out paper plans for the protection of those in authority.

In the practical relations between Short and Kimmel we find the same stupidity as existed between the sections of the general staff of the Army in Washington. Short made no inquiry of Kimmel to determine to what extent Kimmel was carrying out his part of the agreement to conduct distant reconnaissance. Short testified that this was a function of Kimmel into which he did not think it proper for him to inquire. Kimmel likewise relied upon Short to do the things which Short was supposed to do. Again, we were faced with the prerogative jealousy that is guarded so carefully and protected so completely in our services.

Notwithstanding all of the above, it is my belief that the most cordial relation existed between the two commanders. Charges that they were not on speaking terms are in conflict with all of the evidence that our Board obtained.

Naval Intelligence

Much has been said about the statement of now Admiral McMorris. He was in a conference with Kimmel and Short at the time he was head of Kimmel's Naval Intelligence, and was supposed to be familiar with the location of the Japanese Navy, and the probable intentions of the Japanese nation. When he was asked by Admiral Kimmel if an attack by the Japanese forces at Pearl Harbor was anticipated or likely, he replied most emphatically that no such thing could be expected. The Board questioned him about this conclusion but was unable to obtain any bases for such prognostication. The officer merely waved the entire matter aside by saying that he was wrong, and that was that.

This estimate of the Japanese situation by Naval Intelligence is difficult to understand in the light of other events that transpired in the year 1941. In the early part of 1941 some of the Naval officers at Pearl Harbor made an inspection of the Army plans for the defense of the fleet when in the harbor. As a result of this inspection, a memorandum was prepared by the Secretary of Navy and sent to the Secretary of War. In that memorandum the Secretary of the Navy pointed out to the Secretary of War that in the event of a conflict with Japan we might expect an attack at Pearl Harbor by carrier-borne aircraft. The Secretary of Navy regarded this as the most probable form of an attack on the Pacific fleet. The Secretary of Navy was very critical of the provisions that had been made by the Army for the defense of Pearl Harbor. He pointed out in the memorandum the inadequacy of the measures that had been taken by the Army. In reply to this the Secretary of War sent the Secretary of Navy another memorandum. In substance, it stated that the Army was doing the best that it could. The Secretary of War contended that the Army was fully aware of the threat that had been described in the memorandum to the Secretary of the Navy, to wit, an attack by carrier-borne aircraft.

This exchange of documents between the Secretary of War and the Secretary of Navy recognized quite fully the danger from an attack at Pearl Harbor by carrier-borne aircraft. In the light of subsequent developments, it may well be that this exchange of memoranda was the same old service game of each of the departments getting themselves on paper for protective purposes.

In the extensive documents that had been prepared by the two services on the islands for the defense of American interests in the islands, there was an estimate of the situation made by high-ranking officers. In this estimate it was stated that the most probable form of attack would be by carrier-borne aircraft.

In the correspondence between Marshall and Short, it will be remembered the same conclusion was reached.

No good reason was ever found for the abandonment of this estimate on Japanese intentions. One is led to believe that all of the prognostications were paper conclusions, in which those making them had little faith. Everything else at the time of the attack pointed with great emphasis to an invasion to the south of Japan. The probabilities of the Pearl Harbor attack had disappeared.

The war warning message sent by the Navy to Kimmel on the 27th of November, 1941, stated, "An amphibious expedition against either the Philippines, Thai, or Kra Peninsula or possibly Borneo is indicated by the number and equipment of Japanese troops and the organization of their naval task forces." Everybody had forgotten Pearl Harbor but the Japanese and this notwithstanding the fact that one of the intercepted messages had specifically requested information about the part of the Pacific fleet that was based at Pearl Harbor. The conclusion is inevitable that Naval Intelligence was inefficient and the conclusions reached by it were hopelessly unsound. This accounts for the abandonment of all of the earlier interests in the defense of Pearl Harbor.

The reconnaissance that was conducted by the Navy in furtherance of its agreement to assume responsibility for distant reconnaissance has been the subject of frequent debate. The paper plans assigned this function to the Army, but since the Army was without necessary aircraft for the purpose, the Navy took over. The Navy had some aircraft that could be used on that type of reconnaissance. It was never very clear just how many effective planes the Navy had. The very material and pertinent fact is that the Navy was not conducting any reconnaissance, hence was not using such planes as it had. There are confused statements about aircraft on carriers that accompanied maneuvering forces searching for elements of the Japanese Navy, but this was not the type of reconnaissance contemplated. At one place or another reference has been made to a "dawn patrol." It is a beautiful, high-sounding term, but no such thing existed. Apparently there was a minimum of 90 planes that could have been used by the Navy for this reconnaissance. One of the Army witnesses testified that after the attack, he saw the remains of all of these planes at Ford Island. It was here that their planes were based. The Army witness drew the conclusion that not one single plane had been up on the morning of December 7, for the purpose of discovering hostile forces. The Navy and the Army both were not alert, but were taking life very easy when the attack came.

This chapter about the Navy is being written for clarification only. The Army Pearl Harbor Board was not primarily concerned with derelictions of duty by Naval officers. When our investigation of the relations between the Army and Navy at Pearl Harbor had been finished, I was impressed that the personal relations between Short and Kimmel were very cordial, but that no plan for the integration of the efforts of the two staffs had been worked out. Nevertheless, much progress had been made toward the cooperation of the two forces.

7 | The President and the State Department

The President

Early in our deliberations, General Grunert had inquired as to the attitude of General Frank and me toward the President, in event it should develop that some act or failure to act on his part was responsible for the disaster at Pearl Harbor or contributed to it. This has been discussed elsewhere in the story and it will be recalled that an agreement was reached that in event derelictions by the President were indicated, we would submit the evidence establishing these to the President and request any statement that he might care to make. We never found in our investigation the slightest indication that the President interfered with the command of the Army or Navy forces charged with the defense of Pearl Harbor. In making this statement, it should be emphasized that the Army Pearl Harbor Board did not have time to examine in detail the Naval command nor was such examination within the purview of its investigation. There was no doubt that the President left the War Department free in its planning for the defense at Pearl Harbor.

It was equally as evident that the President was intensely interested in negotiations between our Government and the Japanese Empire. Mr. Hull's book, *Peace and War*, has numerous descriptions of conversations between the President and Nomura in 1941, and with Nomura and Kurusu, after the latter's arrival in Washington. Frequently the Japanese envoys would ask for a conference with the President, which indicated that they regarded the President as the dominant figure in the conduct of our international relations. Notwithstanding all of this, I was impressed that Mr. Hull played a very considerable and important part in our negotiations with the Japanese envoys, and exerted a great influence on the decisions made with respect to them. Certain it is that he spoke with apparent authority in the last days of the negotiations.

In our investigation, we found nothing that remotely suggested the necessity of a visit to the President. In our discussion of the Secretary of State, it should be borne in mind that he acted with the consent and approval of the President.

Secretary of State

In the Board's conclusions, Mr. Hull, as Secretary of State, was criticized very mildly. It was my opinion that all reference to the Secretary of State could have been eliminated from these conclusions. I was not fully convinced when the conclusions were being prepared, and now doubt that anything that the Secretary of State did contributed in any substantial way to the disastrous defeat at Pearl Harbor. Such arguments as I made in exoneration of the State Department from blame for the military disaster were not convincing to the others.

One cannot read Mr. Hull's book without being thoroughly convinced that the State Department maintained a firm attitude in its relations with the Japanese, and this is a very charitable description.

Let's explore the record very briefly, as it is set forth in Mr. Hull's book. We must have a beginning point, since any description of our relations with the Japanese covering all of those events which led us into War would be a volume of considerable length in itself.

July 23, 1941, will serve very well as a point of beginning. On that date we find Ambassador Nomura in conversation with Acting Secretary of State Welles. Mr. Hull was sick. Nomura was discussing with Secretary Welles the plan of the Japanese Government to move its armed forces into French Indo-China. If such steps were taken they involved sending Japanese troops much farther to the south than they had previously been. This movement of Japanese troops would be in the direction of Dutch-British possession. Nomura told Welles that he was not informed officially, but had heard that Japan had concluded a treaty with the Vichy Government permitting it to occupy the French possession. Nomura was careful to state that, personally, he was against this operation. Acting for his Government and officially, he attempted to justify the seizing of the French possession on the theory that an underground movement, hostile to the Japanese, was taking place in the area to be occupied by the Japanese. He also said that it was necessary for Japan to seize this part of the continent so that it might have access to rice, oil and other things upon which Japan depended for its protection and existence.

Mr. Welles told Nomura, in substance, that he didn't believe anything that the Japanese had said—that the agreement for the entry into French Indo-China by the Japanese resulted from pressure of the Germans on the French—that it was unnecessary for Japan to seize the territory to insure the flow of supplies it wanted, and further that the alleged threat to Japan by hostile operations in Indo-China would not be taken seriously by us. Welles told Nomura that we could only assume that the occupation of Indo-China by Japan constituted notice to the United States that the Japanese Government intended to pursue a policy of force and of conquest.

The next day, July 24, 1941, we find the Japanese Ambassador Nomura in conference with the President. The Ambassador had requested this conference. Nothing new occurred. It was a virtual rehashing of the talk between Welles and Nomura. It is interesting, however, to note that the President told Nomura that he was permitting the sale of oil to Japan from United States sources, to the end that there would be no need for the Japanese to take over the British and Dutch oil fields in the Pacific. The following statement of the President to Nomura on this occasion defines our foreign policy at that time in a very emphatic way. The President said, "that if Japan attempted to seize oil supplies by force in the Netherlands East Indies, the Dutch would, without the shadow of a doubt, resist; the British would immediately come to their assistance, war would then result between Japan, the British and the Dutch, and in view of our own policy of assisting Great Britain, an exceedingly serious situation would immediately result." This language put the Japanese on notice that if they went to war with Britain they might expect us to come in, and start shooting.

The Japanese moved into Southern Indo-China despite all of the protests and warnings of the President and Secretary of State. Thereupon we attempted to break off negotiations with the Japanese Empire and at the same time froze Japanese assets in this country and placed certain embargoes on the shipment of American materials to Japan.

Negotiations took place between our representatives and the Japanese Ambassador from time to time. The Japanese continued to insist on talking with us, and made numerous representations about their good faith in these conversations.

On the 8th day of August, 1941, Nomura, while exchanging papers with our Secretary of State, asked whether it might not be possible for the responsible heads of the two governments to meet, and suggested Honolulu as the meeting place. The indicated purpose of the meeting was a discussion of the relations between the two governments in an effort to work out some sort of an adjustment. From time to time this matter was pressed by the Japanese representatives. They desired the meeting, they said, as they believed that the publicity given it would dramatize such agreements as might be made and this in turn would strengthen the position of the party in Japan which was favorable to peace, and weaken the position of the war party. Our Government was never friendly to this meeting, although it has been stated that when the matter was mentioned to the President he was not only favorable but was somewhat enthusiastic about it. Nevertheless this willingness of the President, if it existed, came to naught because of the hostility of the State Department to the proposed meeting. The State Department took the position that before any meeting could be held it would be necessary for the agreements, which were to be made at such meeting, to be reached and definitely understood. In other words, there would be no purpose for the meeting except to ratify the agreements previously made. Of course, it would focus the attention of the World on the fact that the two governments were getting together. Personally, I have never understood the position which the State Department took in this matter unless it believed that the Japanese were so anxious for peace with the United States Government that under no conditions would they go to war. We shall return to this statement at a later time.

On the 17th day of August, 1941, the President told Nomura that, "The measures then being taken by the Japanese Government (referring to the seizure of Indo-China) had served to remove the basis for further conversations relative to a peaceful settlement in the Pacific area." Four days later, and on the 21st day of August, 1941, the President reported to Congress on his meeting with Churchill. At that meeting the Atlantic Charter, whatever it may be, came into being.

At this time the pattern of our relations with the Japanese Government was very clear and the demands which we were making on the Japanese took definite form. They were three in number, and from this time until Mr. Hull's note of November 26, it was around these three demands that all of the conversations turned. They were:

1. The Tripartite Pact—This was the agreement for mutual assistance between Germany, Italy and Japan. We demanded that Japan abandon her relations with Germany and Italy as established by this Pact.
2. We insisted that Japan take all of her troops out of China.
3. We demanded that Japan have no favorable trade agreements in the Orient. In other words, all nations must fare alike in the commercial relations with the countries surrounding Japan.

Mr. Hull, in a conversation with Nomura, at the Secretary's apartment, recognized these three points as being of the greatest importance, and emphasized the necessity of Japan's withdrawing from China. Negotiations continued. A lot of papers were exchanged between Nomura and the State Department. Nothing was being accomplished by these memoranda.

On the 29th of September, 1941, Nomura handed Mr. Hull a written statement. In this statement, a meeting between the head of the Japanese Government and the President of the United States was again discussed. The Prime Minister of Japan, Prince Konoye, was pressing for the meeting, and Nomura contended that the willingness of the Prime Minister to go out of the country on a diplomatic mission, which would be the first time that such a thing had occurred in Japanese history, was sufficient testimony of the sincerity of the Japanese Government to settle all of the disputes with our country. In this document, we find a strengthening of the Japanese attitude toward our Government and a very explicit warning. It is contained in the following language: "Eager as we are for peace, we will not bow under the pressure of another country, nor do we want peace at any price. It is a characteristic trait of our people to repel, rather than to submit to, external pressure." After this meeting, there were a lot of words exchanged, much argument back and forth with extensive protestations of good faith on the part of our State Department and the Japanese. Over and over again the three points upon which we were insisting were discussed, but the relations between the two governments increased in tenseness, and the inevitability of war was very obvious, so much so, as a matter of fact, that in November our Government determined that the country must be awakened to the imminence of war. In its efforts to warn the American people of war's approach, Mr. Knox, the Secretary of Navy, spoke at Providence, R. I., on the 11th of November, 1941, and on the same day Mr. Welles, the Undersecretary of State, spoke at Washington. Taking advantage of this Armistice Day, these two speakers pointed to the great events that were immediately before us. Mr. Welles referred to the fact that, "The American people thus have entered the Valley of Decision." Dramatically, he asked, "Can we afford again to refrain from lifting a finger until gigantic forces of destruction threaten all of modern civilization, and the raucous voice of a criminal paranoiac, speaking as the spokesman for these forces from the cellar of a Munich beer hall, proclaims as his set purpose the destruction of our own security, and the annihilation of religious liberty, of political liberty, and of economic liberty throughout the earth?"

One cannot read the two speeches of Secretary Knox and Mr. Welles without knowing that our Government had reached a decision to go to war, if necessary, to prevent the victory of Germany and, of course, the destruction of Japan, Germany's ally, would be a part of the plan.

During this period, Mr. Grew, our Ambassador to Japan, was warning of the rising war spirit of the Japanese people, and emphasizing the need to guard against sudden Japanese naval or military actions in such areas as were not then involved in the Chinese theater of operations. The air was charged with war and every one seemed to know it, except our overseas commanders, who were in the most critical and important of all positions.

On the 18th day of November, 1941, after Kurusu had arrived in this country, and at a time when Tojo had succeeded to the premiership of Japan, Mr. Hull conferred with Nomura and Kurusu. At the meeting the Secretary said, "That he frankly did not know whether anything could be done in the matter of reaching a satisfactory agreement with Japan; that we can go so far but rather than go beyond a certain point it would be better for us to stand and take the consequences."

After rehashing much that had been said, including a rather full discussion of Japanese relations with Germany, Mr. Kurusu told Mr. Hull, "That a comprehensive solution cannot be worked out immediately, that he could make no promises." He said, "That our freezing regulations had caused impatience in Japan and a feeling that Japan had to fight while it still could." Again we find the Japanese representatives expressly threatening us with war.

In this same conversation of November 18, Mr. Hull asked the Japanese representatives how many soldiers the Japanese wanted to retain in China. To this the Ambassador replied that "Possibly 90% would be withdrawn." Mr. Hull then wanted to know how long the Japanese intended to keep the remaining 10% in China. On this question the Japanese representative quibbled, stating that under the Boxer Protocol, Japan was permitted to retain troops in the Peiping and Tientain areas.

This conversation on the 18th of November indicated that both the American and Japanese who were engaged in these negotiations were somewhat irritable. Probably the long talks with little results were producing frayed nerves. At one point when Kurusu was pressing about our removing trade restrictions, he asked if America wanted the status quo ante restored, or what we expected Japan to do. To this Mr. Hull replied that if the Japanese could not do

anything now on those three points—getting troops out of China—
the commercial policy, and the Tripartite agreement, he could only
leave to Japan what Japan could do. This was an emphatic statement
from Mr. Hull that before Japan could expect any concession from
us she must comply with our wishes about these three cardinal
points. To understand clearly our diplomatic relations with the
Japanese, these three points must be kept continuously in mind.

In this plain talk, Mr. Hull told Nomura and Kurusu that the
Japanese Government was responsible for creating the condition
with which the meeting was trying to deal.

In all events our relations were heading toward a climax. Something had to be done or war would come.

On the 20th of November, 1941, the Japanese Ambassador gave
the Secretary of State a written proposal containing conditions for
the settlement of the trouble in the Pacific. Kurusu and Nomura
followed up the delivery of this document with a conversation on the
22nd of November, 1941. Briefly, the Japanese proposed to go no
further to the south and to withdraw its troops from French Indo-
China when agreements were reached or the Chinese War settled. If
temporary arrangements could be worked out in line with the
Japanese plans, it would withdraw troops in Southern Indo-China to
Northern Indo-China. The other main point in the Japanese plan
dealt with its procurement of supplies from the South Pacific.

On the 26th of November, Kurusu and Nomura were in conversation with Mr. Hull. In that conversation, Mr. Hull discussed with
the Japanese representatives a written reply to the Japanese note of
the 20th. This reply of Mr. Hull's was referred to in the Army Pearl
Harbor Board report. It was regarded as an ultimatum by the
Japanese Government. It is the document described by President
Roosevelt in his conversation with Mr. Stimson on the morning of
November 27. The President, it will be recalled, said, in substance,
that the negotiations with the Japanese had ended, but that Cordell
had sent them a fine paper as such negotiations ended.

In this memorandum of November 26, Mr. Hull described ten
things that Japan and the United States would undertake to do.
These ten points constituted a plan for the settlement of all disputed
questions in the Pacific area. Notwithstanding that Mr. Hull set out

ten points in lieu of his original three, there was little new in the memorandum. It included those things that the President and the Secretary had thought should be accomplished to establish friendly relations between the Japanese Empire and our Government. Apparently some of it was acceptable to the Japanese representatives. It was discussed by Kurusu with the Secretary of State before being sent to Japan. But Mr. Kurusu was very clear and emphatic in his denunciation of the plan as a whole. He referred particularly to points three and four of the plan. Point three provided that the Government of Japan will withdraw all military, naval, air and police forces from China and from Indo-China.

Point four provided that the Government of the United States and the Government of Japan will not support—militarily, politically, economically—any government or regime in China other than the National Government of the Republic of China with capital temporarily at Chungking.

In discussing these two points, Mr. Kurusu told Mr. Hull that, "He did not see how his government could consider paragraphs 3 and 4 of the proposed agreement, and that if the United States should expect that Japan was to take off its hat to Chiang Kai-shek and propose to recognize him, Japan could not agree." Proceeding, he said, "That if this was the idea of the American Government, he did not see how any agreement was possible."

Mr. Hull then asked Kurusu if the matter could not be worked out. Kurusu replied that, "When they reported our answer (referring to the 10 points) to their Government it would be likely to throw up its hands."

Further discussing Mr. Hull's memorandum of the 26th, Kurusu said, "That he felt that our response to their proposal could be interpreted as tantamount to meaning the end, and asked whether we were not interested in a modus vivendi." Mr. Hull replied to this proposal of Kurusu for a temporary agreement, that he had explored that. Kurusu asked him if he was against the temporary agreement because other powers would not agree. Mr. Hull said he had done his best in the way of exploration. Here Kurusu was implying that our foreign policies were dominated by others.

It will be remembered that on the next morning, the 27th of November, the evidence indicates, the Japanese task forces sailed from Tankan Bay to attack Pearl Harbor.

On the 29th of November, Mr. Hull talked to the British Ambassador, telling him that our diplomatic relations with Japan were virtually over and that the matter would go to the officials of the Army and Navy to whom he had already talked. In the light of all that happened, it is difficult for me to understand why Mr. Hull gets so disturbed when his memorandum of the 26th is referred to as "an ultimatum."

In the interim between November 26 and December 7, the Japanese representatives were continuing to talk with Mr. Hull and the President. A conversation between the Japanese and Mr. Hull occurred on December 1. In that conversation Kurusu again threatened us with War. Here is the threat in Kurusu's language: "The Japanese people feel that they are faced with the alternative of surrendering to the United States, or of fighting—that he was still trying to save the situation." The next day, and on December 2, Mr. Welles, the Undersecretary of State, talked with Nomura and Kurusu. Mr. Hull was sick again. In this conversation Kurusu repeated his warning that the Japanese would fight us rather than yield to American pressure. His language was, "He did not wish to enter into a debate on the matter, (referring to our freezing measures) but he wished to point out that the Japanese people believe that economic measures are a much more effective weapon of war than military measures; that they believe they are being placed under severe pressure by the United States to yield to the American position; and that it is preferable to fight rather than to yield to pressure."

On December 5, Mr. Hull talked with Mr. Kurusu again, charging that Japan was aiding Hitler by keeping large forces of this country and other countries immobilized in the Pacific area.

On the 6th of December, 1941, the President sent Emperor Hirohito a message. In that message occurs the surprising and startling language, "Thus a withdrawal of the Japanese forces from Indo-China would result in the assurance of peace throughout the whole of the South Pacific area." Mr. Grew testified that this message was probably never delivered to the Emperor.

We do not understand why the President told the Emperor that the withdrawal of Japanese troops from Indo-China would preserve peace in the Pacific. Previously, and on many occasions, Mr. Hull had insisted on the three points: Japanese troops were to get out of China; Japan must break with Germany and Italy; commercial freedom in the Orient must be established. It will be recalled that this positive statement had been made as late as November 18, only eighteen days before the President's message to the Emperor. At that time Mr. Hull had told the Japanese that if they wouldn't agree to the three points it was up to them to do what they could do. Now, two of the points are completely abandoned by the President, and the greater part of the third one is likewise deserted. We abandon two and two third points and cling to one-third of one point.

I have conjectured a lot about this changed attitude. It may well be that the somewhat uncompromising position taken by Mr. Hull in which apparently he had the support of the President was predicated on the intercepted Japanese messages. In all of these messages, Nomura, in the beginning, and later Kurusu and Nomura, after Kurusu arrived in this country, were pressed vigorously by the Japanese Government to conclude some sort of agreement with the United States, which would eliminate us from the war in the South Pacific. It was abundantly clear that the Japanese did not want to fight us. The President and the Secretary of State, knowing that attitude on the part of the Japanese, very probably felt that they could force the Japanese to do what he wanted done, without exposing us to war. It is my further conjecture that on the 5th of December the "Winds" message was received, telling us that Japan had decided to make war on Britain and us. When the President realized that we must go to War, he abandoned the greater part of our previous demands on the Japanese. On no other basis have we been able to explain this retreat on the part of the President, and his willingness to abandon most of his demands.

The above brief description of our relations with the Japanese Government in the fall of 1941 is sufficient to show that war was drawing nearer day by day. A lot has been omitted. If the omitted parts were included here, they would merely corroborate and emphasize the things that have been said.

What the State Department Told the War and Navy Departments

In our study of the State Department, we found a letter that had been sent to the Roberts Commission by the Secretary of State, Mr. Hull. That letter told the Roberts Commission that Mr. Hull had kept the War and Navy Departments fully informed of all the details of the negotiations between our State Department and the representatives of the Japanese Empire. His apparent purpose was to give the Army and Navy the benefit of everything he knew, to the end that they might prepare themselves for such contingencies as the negotiations foretold.

Our study of Mr. Hull's book and the consideration of some of the evidence before the Board, particularly that of Admiral Kimmel, influenced the Board to address a letter to Secretary Hull, through Secretary of War Stimson, in which Mr. Hull's attention was called to the testimony, and he was requested to submit to the Board any further statements about the relations between the War and Navy Departments that he might desire. Mr. Hull replied that the note of November 26 to the Japanese Government was not an ultimatum. He stated further that the State Department did not interfere with the War Department and the Navy Department in their operations. In that letter the Secretary of State made it perfectly clear that he had despaired of accomplishing anything through negotiations with the Japanese Government, but he was extremely anxious to exhaust every method of peaceful settlement to avoid the tragedy of a Japanese attack. It was this that prompted him to send the memorandum of November 26, 1941. His letter to the Board added very little to the letter that he had sent to the Roberts Commission.

Upon the return of the Board to Washington, plans were formulated for calling Mr. Hull as a witness. Before taking this step, the Board sent me to talk with the Secretary of State to determine what testimony we might expect from him, and plan for a visit to his office to take his testimony if we thought wise to call him as a witness.

On this visit I was accompanied by Col. H. A. Toulmin, who was on duty then as Executive of the Army Pearl Harbor Board.

We had a very frank and satisfactory talk with the Secretary of State. He discussed his negotiations with the representatives of the Japanese Empire, following in the main the description of such negotiations contained in his book. He referred to the book on one or more occasions, saying he regarded its publication as unusual in that such things were usually published a long time after the events that they described had occurred. He told us of his conversation with the Secretaries of War and Navy on the morning of the 25th, when he informed them that they might expect war at any time as he had exerted all possible measures in an effort to avoid war. It was in this conversation that Mr. Hull pointed out to the Secretary of War and the Navy that the Armed Forces might expect Japan to resort to bold moves if war came. It was Mr. Hull's belief, as then expressed, that the Japanese recognized that their course of unlimited conquest was a desperate gamble and required the utmost boldness and risk. He expected an attack over considerable areas and the capture of positions and posts throughout the Pacific. He was much wiser and a much better strategist than our high Army and Navy command.

I recall most vividly one incident in our talk with Mr. Hull. He was discussing the broad policy followed by the State Department in his relations with the Japanese Empire. He stated there were men in Washington who thought that we should withdraw from the far Pacific and establish our most distant outpost at Hawaii. We would then permit developments in the Orient without intervention or interference by us. He regarded this view as unsound. It was his belief that Japan would dominate the Orient and with her philosophy of aggression and expansion would be a constant threat to the security of our nation when she had acquired sufficient strength through the conquests upon which she was about to embark. In discussing this tremendously important subject, Mr. Hull stated, "I passed over the contentions of those who advised a withdrawal to Hawaii and looked to the ultimate safety of our country." Mr. Hull was an impressive figure as he arched his long fingers, graphically representing his mental operations in passing over the narrow view of others.

After leaving Mr. Hull's office I gave considerable thought to our talk with him, and what he had written to us and to the Roberts Commission. I discussed it with other members of the Board, telling them we could get nothing new from Mr. Hull by calling him to testify. He was at that time in a very bad way physically, and seemed almost exhausted when he had finished talking with Col. Toulmin and me. I have followed his testimony before the Congressional Committee, and think that our decision not to call him as a witness, was wise.

Our Conduct of Our International Relations

The remaining paragraphs in this chapter have no relation to our investigation of the Pearl Harbor disaster. There are observations that I believe are pertinent, and extremely material in our national life.

I was amazed at the very great power exercised by the President of the United States through the State Department in our foreign relations. It had been my impression that the Congress, in the exercise of its duty created by the Constitution, to make war and provide for the National Defense, played a considerable part in our dealings with other powers. I had heard candidates for the Congress discuss with great vigor and at some length their views on our international relations, as if the Congress had something to do with them.

It was a terrible shock to me, therefore, when I followed our negotiations with the Japanese Empire and discovered the very great freedom with which the President and the Secretary of State conducted negotiations without, insofar as I was able to tell, informing Congress of what was in progress. The Congress, insofar as it influenced the negotiations, might as well have stayed at home. It is not intended to imply that the decisions of the President and the Secretary of State, in their dealings with the Japanese Empire were unsound, but in my opinion nothing in our national life is more dangerous than to vest in one man or even two men the power to

negotiate with other nations freely and without the slightest limitation. It is not difficult to visualize a condition in the future when the
dominant figure may be the President of the United States,
ambitious and looking forward to his position in history. Such a man
could very easily lead us into war.

I have seen young Americans in two wars. One of my last official
acts before returning to civil life was a visit to some general hospitals.
Here I saw scores of boys paralyzed in their lower limbs and unable
to move themselves around because of bullet wounds which they had
received in different parts of the spine. Elaborate appliances had been
purchased and extensive plans made to aid these boys in recovering
from the wounds that they had received. They were bright-eyed and
eager, but very pathetic figures as they struggled with ropes and
rolled about on mats in their efforts to get well.

The things seen in hospitals throughout the country today are but
a small part of the sufferings and sacrifices of war. The tremendous
price which our people must pay in life and in suffering, together
with the almost complete destruction of our economic system, are
too great to be brought about through the decisions of any one
man, or any two or three men. It is to be hoped that the Congress
that is elected by the people and directly responsible to the people
will reassert itself in this tremendously important thing of making
war.

The details of the negotiations with representatives of foreign
powers must be left with some agency of our Government, i.e., The
State Department, but the formulation of broad policies—"For what
must our boys die"—should be vested in those who are nearer to the
people.

8 | Conclusion

Preliminary

The investigation of the Pearl Harbor disaster had presented to the Board many problems and some difficulties. These have been described or can be easily seen from the foregoing chapters of this story. There was nothing difficult about reaching conclusions. They were perfectly obvious, so much so, as a matter of fact, that they shouted at the investigators.

Writing the conclusions down was not a pleasant task. I am quite sure that Generals Grunert and Frank approached this part of the work with a full realization of its probable effect on the future of their military careers. As was said in Chapter 1 of this book, both of these officers were holding temporary ranks in the expanded army, considerably higher than the ranks that they held on the permanent list. Criticism of the War Department that meant criticism of Marshall, the Chief of Staff, was inescapable. This was not debatable. Throughout the military service Marshall was regarded as not only ruthless but intensely vindictive. He was intolerant of the views of everyone but himself, and those who dared disagree with him might expect to feel the full force of his vengeance.

It must be said, therefore, to the great credit and courage of Grunert and Frank that they helped to write the story, as it was told by the witnesses, and did not flinch in drawing accurate and truthful conclusions.

For my part, I was not interested in Marshall's opinion of me. There was nothing that he could do to or for me that concerned me in the least. Nevertheless I was a member of the Armed Forces of the United States, with more than 28 years of service as a National Guardsman, almost nine of which had been in the field. My experience in World War II had destroyed a great part of the respect that I previously had for the professional soldier. Notwithstanding this fact, I realized that the faith of the people of the United States in its Army and Navy was one thing that must be maintained. General Grunert, General Frank and I were all of that Army. I was as much interested in the future of the Army as any officer in it. The criticisms that we must write might go far to undermine such faith as the great masses of the people still had in the Army. I approached the preparation of the conclusions with a sense of dread, and so far as I know this same feeling was entertained by both Generals Frank and Grunert.

General

The operations of our Armed Forces in the face of Japanese threats had been so weak and unintelligent as to be downright depressing. The imminence and inevitability of war during the fall of 1941 were perfectly evident to any one who knew the facts. It could not be denied that both the War and Navy Departments were acquainted with these developments in their minutest details. Contrary to the general impression, the Japanese were not stringing us along, attempting to lull us into a sense of security. They were telling us in the very plainest of language that they would fight before they would permit us to dominate the Orient and dictate the Japanese course in that area. Not only that, but from the things that the representatives of the Japanese Empire said to us openly and the information which we secured from the intercepted messages, we knew or should have known very early in the fall that unless an agreement was reached between us and the Japanese Empire before the end of 1941, war would come.

We had probably placed too great reliance on the intense desire of the Japanese Empire to keep us neutral while they launched their campaigns of conquest down the Malayan Peninsula, against the Dutch possessions, and into Australia. The struggle between the Japanese on the one hand and the British and Dutch, aided by the weak Chinese Nation on the other, appeared inescapable. Those responsible for our international policy told the Japanese that we would not tolerate this development and the Army and Navy were informed immediately by the State Department of this attitude.

Notwithstanding all of the above, when the Japanese struck, at dawn on the morning of December 7, 1941, they found our Army and Navy forces literally asleep. But this wasn't all. The War Department knew that the Army forces were not alerted for an attack at Pearl Harbor. There was a complete, utter and dismal failure of those forces in Hawaii, both Army and Navy, to make an effort to accomplish their mission of maintaining an outpost at Pearl Harbor for the protection of the west coast of the United States and preserving American interests in the Pacific.

Parenthetically, I might say that the Army Pearl Harbor Board knew little of naval dispositions at Pearl Harbor. In the light of testimony before the Congressional Committee, now in session, it seems that Stark had directed Kimmel to make defensive deployments that in Navy language had a real meaning and required that Kimmel not withdraw to Pearl Harbor as he did.

These inescapable general facts required that the Army Pearl Harbor Board go further and analyze the evidence produced, both oral and documentary, to the end that derelictions of responsible officers might be segregated and described. We shall, in writing these personal conclusions, follow the general pattern of the story that has just been finished.

The War Department

General Marshall and his associates in the War Department must rely for vindication on the message of November 27, 1941, (472). Whatever may be the arguments made by them, they must realize the truth of this statement. In Mr. Stimson's condemnation of the Army Pearl Harbor Board referred to in the preface to this story, he stated that General Short had been "clearly warned on November 27 by the appropriate authorities in Washington that a break in diplomatic relations between the United States and Japan might occur at any time, that an attack by Japan on the United States might occur, and that hostilities were possible at any moment."

Recently, General Marshall in his testimony before the Congressional Committee stated that he had given Short definite and specific instructions, and he expected that these instructions would be carried into effect. He attempted to justify himself and his conduct, prior to the Pearl Harbor attack, by saying that it was the policy of the War Department to estimate information in its possession, reach conclusions and notify field commanders of such conclusions, in short, specific, definite orders.

If Short had such an order and failed to follow it, and by reason of such failure Pearl Harbor resulted, he cannot be too strongly condemned, or too severely punished. This brings us, therefore, to a consideration of the message of November 27, 1941, and the action that was taken on this message by Short in Hawaii, and Marshall in Washington. The message is:

No. 472. Negotiations with Japanese appear to be terminated to all practical purposes with only the barest possibilities that the Japanese Government might come back and offer to continue. Japanese future action unpredictable but hostile action possible at any moment. If hostilities cannot, repeat cannot, be avoided, the U. S. desires that Japan commit the first overt act. This policy should not, repeat not, be construed as restricting you to a course of action that might jeopardize your defense. Prior to hostile Japanese action, you are directed to undertake such reconnaissance and other measures as you deem necessary but these measures should be carried out so as not, repeat not, to alarm the civil population or disclose intent. Report measures taken. Should hostilities occur, you will carry out task assigned in Rainbow Five as far as they pertain to Japan. Limit dissemination of this highly secret information to minimum essential officers.

In order to understand the above message, it must be considered in sections. The first two sentences were placed in it by the Secretary of War, a civilian. They are:

> Negotiations with Japanese appear to be terminated to all practical purposes with only the barest possibility that the Japanese Government might come back and offer to continue. Japanese future action unpredictable but hostile action possible at any moment.

These two sentences are weak, speculative and left much to be desired. Nevertheless, they are the most satisfactory part of the message. They state that we may or may not continue to negotiate with the Japanese and further that Marshall did not know what the Japanese might do, though they might start fighting.

In this connection, it is important to know that the Japanese did come back and did continue to negotiate. Nomura and Kurusu were in conference with the Secretary of State and Mr. Welles three times after November 27. The conversations occurred on the first, second and fifth of December. The fact that these negotiations were being continued was publicized and referred to in the newspapers at Hawaii. It came to pass, therefore, that Short in the Islands, notwithstanding the fact that he had nothing further from Marshall, knew or could have known that the two governments were continuing their negotiations. This knowledge did much to destroy the force of the first two sentences of the message.

When we leave these first two sentences of the order, so completely characterized by uncertainty, we get into the do-don't part of the order. The next two sentences are:

> If hostilities cannot, repeat cannot, be avoided, the U. S. desires that Japan commit the first overt act. This policy should not, repeat not, be construed as restricting you to a course of action that might jeopardize your defense.

In substance, they tell Short that if war comes it is the desire that Japan hit first. In effect he is told not to start a war. The War

Department, to escape responsibility for inactivity on Short's part because of this injunction, then "throws in" the saving sentence that such policy is not to be construed as requiring Short to sit by and be destroyed by aggressive Japanese action. These two sentences constitute a deplorable, self-protecting straddle.

Next follows a jewel of ambiguity and weakness:

> Prior to hostile Japanese action, you are directed to undertake such reconnaissance and other measures as you deem necessary, but these measures should be carried out so as not, repeat not, to alarm the civil population or disclose intent.

Short is told in this sentence to do whatever he desires, including undertaking reconnaissance, but he is to do it very secretively. He is to go to war, in a measure, without letting anybody know about it. His movements were to be made in the presence of almost 200,000 Japanese.

The next sentence: "Report measures taken" is the short sentence of the message, and is very direct. These are the words that have arisen to haunt the War Department because Short told the War Department what he had done, and the War Department by its inactivity approved Short's decision.

The next sentence of the message is not so very important as it refers only to some previous plans for waging war against Japan. It is quoted here for the sake of completeness only:

> Should hostilities occur, you will carry out task assigned in Rainbow Five as far as they pertain to Japan.

The final sentence of the message was crippling in its effect and worked a severe handicap on an officer who was inclined to follow the letter of any instructions given him:

> Limit dissemination of this highly secret information to minimum essential officers.

In our discussion of the conduct of the personnel operating the radar stations on the morning of December 7, we pointed out the vice of this instruction. We found one officer and several enlisted men discharging the most critical function imaginable and not one of them had the slightest inkling of what was contained in this message of November 27. We also cited the garbled report of the message as it was transmitted to a division commander by his aide.

The proper sentence would have been, communicate this highly important information to all essential military personnel. After all, the American soldier is intelligent, and all the wisdom is not confined to the General Staff.

To understand the form and substance of this message, the international situation at the time must be kept constantly in mind and the timidity of the general staff must not be forgotten. The situation in the Pacific was very tense. When Kurusu reached Washington in November 1941, he insisted that something must be done and be done in a hurry, else war would come. He had stopped off at different places on his trip from Japan to Washington. He referred to the situation in the Pacific as a powder keg, meaning, of course, that the slightest incident might be sufficient to set off a great explosion, to wit, war between the United States and the Japanese Empire. The officers in the War Department were or should have been aware of this tenseness. They knew that we were not ready for War and furthermore, that it was the deep desire of the Administration not to commit any act which could be used by the Japanese as a basis for beginning war. Incidents between members of the Armed forces, or demonstrations by troops could constitute such an act. An officer or officers responsible for such an incident or who permitted one, would be on the way out.

Short, in the Islands, was on the outpost and likewise on the spot. He was in command of troops who might commit the overt act. If one such arose Short could attempt justification by saying that he was following instructions contained in the message of November 27. If Short was successful in such contentions it would follow that Marshall, in sending the order, had brought on war.

These are the things behind the jumbled and garbled message. These are the things that account for the limitations and restrictions that were placed on Short. These are the things that account for the great secrecy enjoined in the message. These are the things that render the message valueless and destroy Marshall's defense, insofar as it relies on the message.

Short was a typical army officer. He knew when he received the message that some action was required. He sought the easy way out by ordering the sabotage alert and immediately reporting that to the War Department. Thereupon, he poured the entire mess back into Marshall's lap. This is an inelegant expression, but is accurate and descriptive.

Marshall was caught asleep. He did nothing about it. He awoke at 11.30 A.M., December 7, 1941, when the Japanese planes were almost in flight for Pearl Harbor. He makes no serious contention that he did not see Short's sabotage reply. Others about him have attempted to shield him but he knows the reply passed over his desk and that it was his duty to see it. Stimson's weak contention, that Marshall couldn't be bothered with such matters as he was engaged in planning a global war, is ridiculous. Nothing in the global scene was more important at the time than our relations with the Japanese Empire and the probable outbreak of war in the Pacific. This was the most important thing in our international relations.

There is an explanation of the implied approval of Short's sabotage alert to Marshall which lies in the fact that everyone concerned in the War Department believed War would come on the Kra peninsula and in the areas of the Pacific adjacent thereto. They believed that the only possibility of an attack against us involved the Philippine Islands. All of the testimony is to that effect. When Secretary Stimson sent for the officers on the morning of November 27, it was for the purpose of preparing a message to MacArthur. At 11.30 o'clock on Sunday morning, December 7, Marshall telephoned MacArthur, and sent a telegram to Short.

It was abundantly clear that the War Department had been caught napping. The Board sought for some reasonable explanation for these War Department derelictions. We looked at the Staff. These were the men who had been selected by Marshall as his assistants. They have been referred to already. Among them were some of the older men of the service, indoctrinated with concepts of staff procedure which were outmoded. They were dignified, restrained, theoretical, desk operators. They lacked that practical, common sense which makes for direct intelligent action. Typical of these were Bryden, Deputy Chief of Staff, and Miles, the G-2.

Another type of officer was among Marshall's associates. He was the up and coming younger man from the schools. He represented a departure in our army life. This type of officer is likewise bound by the red tape and the established procedure of the service. He knows a lot that is in the book, but like his older brother, is incapable of intelligent, practical reasoning. He played a great part in World War II. In the War Department in the fall of 1941, we find representatives of this group, Bedell Smith, Secretary to the General Staff, and Gerow, Chief of the War Plans Division. Doubtless these two officers knew all about staff procedure. They were selected because of this knowledge and their training. To me, the outstanding example of their unfitness for their jobs and their incompetence is the refusal of Bedell Smith to give any comfort or aid to Bratton and Sadtler when these two men were pleading for more action from the War Department in its relation with the Overseas Departments. If Gerow was not interested in sending additional information or requiring more alertness in the Overseas Departments, then Marshall was not interested because under the plan of operations in the War Department such matters were the exclusive function of the War Plans Division. If the War Plans Division missed the boat on Short's sabotage reply, then the other sections of the general staff might not interfere because it was not "cricket" for one section of the general staff to invade the province of another section of the general staff. Here was prerogative jealousy rearing its head at a most unfortunate time. In obedience to its demands, the Pacific fleet at Pearl Harbor might be destroyed. Three thousand young Americans might die in a hopeless battle. Years of suffering in the jungles of the South Pacific might follow, but the prerogatives of the staff sections of the War Department must be and they were preserved. This was the important thing.

Marshall was the Chief of this staff, and responsible for the selection of its personnel. I have talked with him at different times and have examined him as a witness on the three occasions described in this story. I have seen him appear before groups of officers and talk to them at other times. I have never seen him yet when he wasn't very busy and anxious to impress those who were listening to him with the strain under which he was laboring, and the great part he was playing in things. My impression of Marshall when related to execution, exclusively, is one of business and bungling. This must not be construed as meaning any qualification of the high opinion that I have of him as a salesman.

I doubt if at any critical time in our history our interests were in the hands of a weaker group of men than those constituting the War Department in December 1941.

The conduct of the War Department from the evening of December 6, 1941, until the time of the attack reflects a state of inefficiency which is so amazing that its description would not be believed were it not so completely established. When the Japanese message announcing the end of negotiations was received on Saturday evening, it went over to the War Department.

Recently a witness who delivered this message to the President described the reaction of the President and Mr. Harry Hopkins, who was with him, to this message. These two civilians knew that this message meant war and war now. The Navy gave the message to the War Department.

Colonel Bratton has wavered in his testimony about delivering the message to the Chief of Staff. From the standpoint of the War Department's responsibility for Pearl Harbor, this is immaterial. The Navy gave it to the War Department and there was no one in the War Department who could or did do anything about it until 11.30 Sunday morning. More than fifteen tragic hours passed during which nothing was done.

Early Sunday morning the last paragraph of this message, together with an order for destroying the code machines of the Japanese, was received. This Japanese memorandum, tantamount to a declaration of war, was to be delivered at 1 P.M. The Navy sent this to the War Department before 9 A.M., Sunday morning, but nothing could be or was done about it until Marshall reached his office at 11.30 A.M. In this story, statements have been made about the charges that Marshall was running the War Department as a one-man show. When the Army Pearl Harbor Board was reaching its conclusions, a finding that General Marshall failed to have some one in the War Department who could act in his absence was inserted into the tentative conclusions. One of the members of the Board asked that this be eliminated since there might be a slight doubt about it. It was stricken from the findings. To me, it is one of the most important of all of the conclusions, that in this critical hour only one man in the War Department could act in so dangerous an emergency. If the horseback ride could not be interrupted, then a Deputy Chief of Staff, other than Bryden, should have been available.

If the "winds" message was received on December 5, we knew then that Japan had reached a definite decision to fight Britain and us. If such message was not received, we knew on Saturday night that Japan had terminated negotiations with us. We knew early Sunday morning that war would come at one o'clock that day, but nothing was done. The War Department was enjoying its weekend of leisure and this could not be disturbed by a little Japanese war. What a sorry picture!

Marshall told Short little that he knew. He approved Short's sabotage alert order. He tolerated a weak staff of incompetents and misfits. He attempted to run a big job on a small plan, and he fired Short for minor derelictions to protect himself against possible destruction for major derelictions.

The Hawaiian Department

The relations between the Hawaiian Department and the War Department were so close that it is difficult to discuss the failures of one without at the same time referring to the failures of the other. They were interlocking.

In Hawaii, Short made the wrong decision. He limited his alert to operations for the prevention of sabotage. He should have made his command ready to repel an attack. He didn't and in this he failed.

He disregarded that portion of the message of November 27 that directed that he take such reconnaissance as he deemed necessary.

The Army Pearl Harbor Board found that this instruction was an order. Such finding was based on a strained construction of the language of the order. Short's failure to have his radar in full operation on the morning of December 7 was a failure.

The testimony about available aircraft to conduct reconnaissance was confused and conflicting. It is impossible to say dogmatically that Short failed in this particular. Here, when Short's failures are examined for justification, or excuse, the investigator enters an uncertain and difficult field.

General Marshall charges that Short was given definite orders that he failed to obey. The Army Pearl Harbor Board could not agree with Marshall and found that the order of November 27 was inadequate. To me, as an individual, it is a fine example of everything that an order should not be.

Short's case in this connection is greatly strengthened, if not completely made out, by his report of action taken, and Marshall's failure to direct a higher form of alert.

At one time or another Marshall has charged that the Pearl Harbor disaster resulted from Short's failure to exercise that sound judgment which is expected of those in high place in the Army. Closely related to this contention of Marshall's is the position which Generals Grunert and Frank maintained from the outset of the investigation, to wit: That Short failed to apply the military principle, to prepare for the worst which the enemy could do to him. These two statements, while somewhat analogous, are not the same.

Marshall's condemnation of Short for failure to exercise the superior judgment required of him by virtue of his rank and assignment is wholly unjustified. Marshall had a high duty to keep Short advised of the trend in world events and the details of our negotiations with the Japanese to the end that Short might have the necessary information to make proper decisions for the employment of his forces. A lieutenant general should not be treated as a corporal and expected to act as a lieutenant general. When Marshall failed to keep Short informed and relied on one single message to accomplish what should have been done, it was incumbent on Marshall to make his instructions to Short definite, specific and clear.

It is impossible for me to understand by any satisfactory line of reasoning why Marshall missed the fact that Short had not properly alerted his troops. Short knew little. Marshall knew much. Short can be excused for his limited alert. Marshall can never be justified in failing to demand a higher form of alert.

The reasoning of Grunert and Frank which found its way into the Board's report is much sounder than the contention of Marshall which has just been discussed.

Paragraph 4 (a) of the Board's conclusion is a fine statement of this dereliction of Short, and is quoted here because of its completeness and accuracy. He failed:

(a) To place his command in a state of readiness for war in the face of a war warning by adopting an alert against sabotage only. The information that he had was incomplete and confusing but it was sufficient to warn him of the tense relations between our Government and the Japanese Empire and that hostilities might be momentarily expected. This required that he guard against surprise to the extent possible and make ready his command so that it might be employed to the maximum and in time against the worst form of attack that the enemy might launch.

Reference has been made to Short's faith in the Navy and his evidence that he did not regard it as proper to inquire into Kimmel's conduct prior to the attack. This attitude of the Services toward each other and the prerogative jealousy within the General Staff is all of the same sorry piece. It is my deep hope that some time we shall have a spirit in the Army and Navy that recognizes that the protection of the interests of the American people is of far greater importance than the maintenance of silly customs of the Services.

I agreed most heartily with the conclusions of the Board that criticized Short's failure to replace inefficient staff officers. I repeat what was said in the body of the story. I don't know how a staff such as the one at Pearl Harbor could have been assembled and held together.

Short made a wrong decision and issued an incorrect order; he was indifferent about reconnaissance; he tolerated a weak staff.

The Navy

In such discussions as I have seen of the Navy's failures in the Pearl Harbor disaster, the principal point has always been missed. The defeat at Pearl Harbor was a Navy defeat. Waiving all of the debates and discussions, and eliminating the mass of details that have grown up around this incident, it remains that a part of the Japanese Navy outguessed, outsmarted and destroyed a substantial part of the American Navy. When this cold fact is stated, everything else becomes relatively unimportant.

I recall that on occasions prior to World War II, high ranking Naval officers stated that the American Navy could destroy the Japanese Navy any Thursday morning before breakfast. Apparently our Navy had a kind of contempt for the Japanese Navy. When war came the Japanese Navy selected Sunday morning, not Thursday morning, and destroyed a substantial part of the American Navy before breakfast.

It is a poor alibi for our naval men to complain of inadequate means for reconnaissance and to attempt to justify the defeat by saying that the equipment of the Japanese Navy was so far superior to that of our own, that defeat was inevitable, either inside of Pearl Harbor or in the open seas. It would be most interesting if some one with the capacity and courage would investigate the development of our Navy prior to World War II to determine why the Japanese Navy was so much more modern and so much more effective than our own. Would this investigation disclose that the money spent on our Navy in those years prior to World War II was wasted because of unwise planning by those charged with the responsibility for designing the type of ships and aircraft for use by our Navy?

Relations between the Army and Navy forces at Pearl Harbor left much to be desired. Short and Kimmel were friendly. The War and Navy Departments and the Army and Navy Forces at Hawaii had prepared a lot of papers that didn't mean much. Staff integration and cooperation were poor.

It is my belief that the answer to all of the confusion at Pearl Harbor is a real unified command of all of our Armed forces.

The failures of Stark in Washington and Kimmel at Pearl Harbor were the same as those of Marshall in Washington and Short at Pearl Harbor, and need not be repeated.

The State Department and the President

Our State Department should be brought in line with other American institutions. Power to make war should be transferred back to Congress, where the Constitution placed it.

The stiff-necked attitude of the President and the Secretary of State toward the Japanese representatives during the fall of 1941 was not wise. We were not fully prepared for war. Not only was there a deficiency in our equipment, but as has been so completely shown by all of the investigations, our Army and Navy were poorly organized and weakly commanded in critical places. Time was of the very essence of the situation. The Japanese were telling us that they would fight if we pressed them too hard. Probably because of the Japanese messages that we were intercepting and reading, we didn't believe these statements. In all events, we repeat, they did not "string us along." The State Department should recognize that it is a part and parcel of the Government and that its international polices must not outrun our preparations for their enforcement by the Army and Navy.

When the Army Pearl Harbor Board was considering its conclusions with respect to the State Department, I insisted on writing into the criticism of the State Department two sentences. They are: "To the extent that it hastened such attack, it was in conflict with the efforts of the War and Navy Departments to gain time for preparations for war. However, war with Japan was inevitable and imminent because of irreconcilable disagreements between the Japanese Empire and the American Government."

It may well be that the attack on us by Japan in 1941 was inevitable, unless we agreed to stay out of the war in the Pacific. Such a situation, however, did not justify the State Department in washing its hands of the entire affair on the 25th of November, 1941. Reason demanded that these negotiations be continued to the end that the Army and Navy might have more time to get ready for war.

Our Intelligence Service

If our intelligence service had functioned, even feebly, we might have known what the Japanese Navy was planning. The Army Pearl Harbor Board recommended that something be done about this. If we are to play our part in international affairs, we should preserve the lives of our young men in the future by acquainting ourselves with World developments. The outlook for an effective Intelligence Service is not good. It is distinctly bad. The personnel of the Army and Navy lack the capacity and energy to organize such service, and make it function. We must have practical, intelligent, aggressive, forceful men, who aren't too good to do the dirty work required. The Army and Navy personnel, of today, will never meet the demand.

In my opinion the State Department is worse. Intelligence work is of the earth, earthy, and is not even remotely related to the stratospheric atmosphere of the State Department.

It is my information that the State, War and Navy Departments are now struggling for the control of our world-wide intelligence service.

9 | Recommendations

The order appointing the Board provided that it would make "such recommendations" as it may deem proper.

Before the investigation was completed, I realized that recommendations would be futile. The action of the Secretary of War, ordering the utmost secrecy about the Board's deliberations and work, indicated very clearly that he was in disagreement with the Board and had decided already that no publicity would be given to our findings. His testimony was convincing that he was "going to bat" for Marshall and himself. He was dominated by Marshall. Had the Board made a recommendation adverse to General Marshall, he, acting through Secretary Stimson, would have disregarded it.

I doubted the propriety of a recommendation for a reorganization of the War Department. The Board had been appointed by an order of the Secretary of War. A recommendation that he and Marshall be given the same treatment that Short received would have been a little presumptuous. We put down the facts and drew the conclusions. The next step was the President's. He didn't need the Board's directions in the nature of recommendations. Personally, I didn't anticipate any executive action. The very contrary was true. I was sure nothing would be done.

When General Short's treatment was considered, I had a feeling of depressed helplessness. I knew that he had been treated outrageously, but the Board could do nothing about it. Relieved from his command for his mistakes, he had been driven out of the Service under a threat of court-martial. He was an old soldier and knew the Army and Marshall. The court-martial would have been appointed by Marshall, who would have been vitally interested in the Court's verdict. Short, along with any other experienced officer in the Army, could have written that verdict before the trial began. He did the wise thing and chose the easy way out. As a practical matter Short's case was closed, unless the Board thought he should be tried by court-martial. So far as I know, no member of the Board thought he should be tried.

General Frank prepared, for the Board's consideration, a very well-worded recommendation. In substance it stated that General Short had received the soldier's greatest punishment, relief from his command and retirement in time of War. Marshall had done a magnificent job and should be forgiven.

This proposed recommendation was not considered favorably.

I believed then and believe now that all those responsible for our defeat at Pearl Harbor should have been dealt with alike. If one was driven out of the Service all should have been. If one was forgiven, all should have been. To select an individual as a sacrifice for the sins of the group was not only unfair, but was downright despicable.

To me the conduct of those in high places, after the attack, was dishonest and inexcusable. A short, frank, understandable statement, disclosing what has occurred would have ended all the controversies about Pearl Harbor. The debates, the criminations and recriminations, the unnecessary investigations, all those would have been avoided. This procedure required a type of courage and character in high places which was wholly lacking.